KNOTTING
AND SPLICING
ROPES AND CORDAGE

KNOTTING
AND SPLICING
ROPES AND CORDAGE

PAUL N. HASLUCK

Skyhorse Publishing

Skyhorse Publishing books may be purchased in bulk at special discounts for sales promotion, corporate gifts, fund-raising, or educational purposes. Special editions can also be created to specifications. For details, contact the Special Sales Department, Skyhorse Publishing, 307 West 36th Street, 11th Floor, New York, NY 10018 or info@skyhorsepublishing.com.

Skyhorse® and Skyhorse Publishing® are registered trademarks of Skyhorse Publishing, Inc.®, a Delaware corporation.

Visit our website at www.skyhorsepublishing.com.

10 9 8 7 6 5

Library of Congress Cataloging-in-Publication Data is available on file.

Cover design by Adam Bozarth

ISBN: 978-1-61608-678-7
Ebook ISBN: 978-1-62087-354-0

Printed in the United States of America

CONTENTS

LIST OF ILLUSTRATIONS

KNOTTING AND SPLICING ROPES AND CORDAGE

CHAPTER I.

INTRODUCTION: ROPE FORMATION.

KNOTTING is an ancient device with which very early inhabitants of this earth must have been acquainted. From the beginning, mankind must always have used some kind of knot to join animal sinews, plant fibres, or hide strips which, in ancient days, were the prototypes of the varieties of cordage now employed.

A large number of knots has been invented by the skill of man, and on their strength and correct tying depend the lives of thousands and thousands of workmen—seamen, building trade operatives, etc., day by day. The importance of being able to make the knot best suited for the occasion both rapidly and correctly may come in a new light to some when it is pointed out that both lives and property have over and over again been sacrificed to ill-made knots; and this little volume is put forward in the belief that few things better repay the workman's time and trouble in learning than the manipulation of ropes and cordage.

Cordage is used almost daily by everyone in some form or other, but comparatively few can handle it methodically. Men break their nails and teeth gnawing at their own knots endeavouring to untie them, and time and material are wasted. Time spent in learning a few of the simple bends and hitches, reliable under strain and easy to unbend when the strain is released, would never be regretted. It is not necessary for a landsman to learn all the numerous uses to which rope is put, but a knowledge of common "bends" is an inestimable convenience, if not a necessity.

The security of a knot ought not to be, as many seem to think, in the number of turns or hitches in its composition, but in the efficacy of the nip. A "bend" or "hitch" must be so formed that the part of rope under strain nips some portion of the knot, either against itself or the object to which it is attached; and in learning a bend, or impressing it upon one's memory, it will be found most helpful to notice particularly the nip of each separate one as it is studied.

Rope, though usually of hemp, is made of other materials for certain purposes. Coir rope (cocoanut fibre), being light and buoyant, is useful for warps, rocket lines, life-buoy lines, and drift-nets. Manilla grass is adapted for reef points, yachts' hawsers, and wherever tar would be injurious. Hide is required for wheel-ropes, or where great strength with pliability and small circumference is needed. Cotton is serviceable for fancy work, etc. The "yarns" are formed by twisting the hemp right-handed; the "strands," by twisting or laying up the yarns left-handed; and the rope, by laying up the strands right-handed.

Three ropes laid up left-handed form what is known as a cable-laid rope; four-stranded ropes are laid round a heart. Ropes are sometimes laid left-handed, but if the strands are to be laid left-handed the yarns are laid right-handed. If the parts of hemp, etc., be twisted more than is necessary to hold them together, strength is lost. Upon following the course of a yarn in a rope it will be found that, by this alternate laying, it runs nearly straight with the direction of the rope's length.

A three-stranded rope will bear a greater strain

in comparison with its size than any other of the same material; cable-laid ropes and four-stranded ropes are, roughly speaking, about one-fifth weaker. Rope is measured by its circumference, and is laid up in lengths of 113 fathoms, sizes varying up to 28 in.; but it is not usually made up in coils when the size exceeds 5 in. Very small ropes are distinguished by their yarns rather than their size; thus sailors speak of nine-, twelve-, and eighteen-yarn stuff, which is commonly called "seizing stuff."

If the fibres of which a rope is composed were laid parallel to one another and fastened at the two ends, the combined strength of these fibres would be utilised to the full; in other words, they lose strength by being twisted or "laid up." But, on the other hand, the length of the fibres being at most but a few feet, their usefulness in this state is very limited, and the inconvenience of using them so is prohibitive. For this reason the fibres are first twisted into "yarns"; these, again, are laid up into "strands," a strand being formed of several yarns; and, finally, three or more strands are formed into a rope. As twisting diminishes the strength of a rope, it is important that the yarns be carefully laid up, so as to bring an even strain on every part. It should not be laid up too hard—that is, it should only have sufficient twist in it to prevent the fibres from being drawn out without breaking.

"Hawser-laid" ropes are made of three strands laid right-handed, or "with the sun," as it is termed. "Shroud-laid" are made of four strands laid right-handed. A "cable-laid" rope is made of three hawser-laid ropes laid up left-handed, and therefore contains nine strands. Obviously the size of a rope is regulated by the quantity of yarns composing the strands, and not by the number of strands that it contains.

With regard to the weight of ropes, it may be said that ropes of all kinds are usually measured by their circumference. The weight of clean, dry, hemp rope in pounds per fathom is one-fourth of the square of the circumference in inches; for example, a 3-in. hemp rope (about 1 in. in diameter) weighs $\frac{1}{4} \times 3^2 = 2\frac{1}{4}$ lb. per fathom (6 ft.). A flat hemp rope, with a width of about four times the thickness, weighs in pounds per fathom about twice the square of the circumference in inches; for example, a 3-in. by $\frac{3}{4}$-in. flat hemp rope will weigh about $2 \times 7 = 14$ lb. per fathom.

Round wire ropes weigh in pounds per fathom seven-eighths of the square of the circumference in inches; for example, a 3-in. wire rope weighs about $\frac{7}{8} \times 3^2 = 7\frac{7}{8}$ lb. per fathom. A flat wire rope weighs in pounds per fathom ten times the sectional area in square inches; for example, a flat wire rope, 3 in. by $\frac{3}{4}$ in. = say 2 sq. in. area, will weigh about $10 \times 2 = 20$ lb. per fathom.

The maximum safe load on a rope depends on many circumstances, such as quality, age and dryness of rope, nature of load, mode of lifting, etc Approximately, the safe load on a new hemp rope in hundredweights with direct lift is three times the weight in pounds per fathom. On a sound old rope fall one-half the square of the circumference is sufficient load. A Bessemer steel wire rope will safely carry in hundredweights three times the square of its circumference in inches, and a crucible steel wire rope four times the square of its circumference. For hemp ropes the minimum diameter of sheave should be circumference of rope + 2, and for wire ropes the diameter of sheave in inches should be equal to circumference of rope in sixteenths.

The principle of rope making is very readily shown by holding the ends of a piece of twine or whipcord, about a foot long, in the hands and twisting it so as to increase the lay. If the twine be now slackened by bringing the hands nearer to one another, a loop will first form in the middle of the twine, and it will continue to twist itself up into a compact cord which will not unlay, as the tension to which the strands have been subjected causes friction between them, which holds them together. In other words, the tendency of each part singly to unlay, acting in opposite directions, is the means of keeping them together when joined.

Some very interesting experiments were made by Reaumur, the purposes of which were to ascertain the loss of strength occasioned by laying up the fibres of various substances, one or two of which are given.

1. A thread, consisting of 832 fibres of silk, each of which carried 1 dram and 18 grains, broke with a weight of 5 lbs., though the sum of the absolute strength of the fibres is 104 drams, or upwards of 8 lbs. 2 oz.

2. Three threads were twisted together, their mean strength being nearly 8 lbs. They broke with $17\frac{1}{2}$ lbs., whereas they should have carried 24 lbs.

These experiments prove that though convenience and portability are gained by twisting the fibres, there is a great loss in the strength of the resultant rope.

In speaking of the size of a rope, the circumference and not the diameter is alluded to. Thus, a three-inch rope would be slightly less than an inch in diameter.

In practising knotting it is as well to use a tolerably firm material, such as whipcord, for small common knots, or, still better, line used for sea fishing. Either can be tied up and undone over and over again without injuring it, which is not the case with twine; it is also more easy to see which way the parts of a knot lie in the harder material, and then to find out whether the turns are properly made or not. For more complicated knots, particularly those where the strands of the rope have to be unlaid to form the knot, such as a wall knot (p. 66) or a Matthew Walker (p. 70), it is advisable to use three strands of fishing line, each about a foot long. If a "seizing" (a seizing is shown in Fig. 57, p. 51) be put round them in the centre, so as to hold them firmly together, a good representation of a rope with the strands unlaid ready for working is obtained. A knot can be made and unmade as often as required in this way, without detriment to the strands; but the strands of a rope, owing to their loose nature, will seldom bear knotting more than once or twice. If desired, the knots can be made as above described and kept for future reference. In string also it is better to use hard laid stuff at first, but when these matters are thoroughly understood knots can be made on any sort of cordage without difficulty.

CHAPTER II.

SIMPLE AND USEFUL KNOTS.

THE simplest knot that is made is the overhand knot (Fig. 1). It is very useful, and forms a part of many other knots. To make it, the standing part of the rope—that is, the main part in opposition to the end—is held in the left hand, and the

Fig. 1.—Overhand Knot.

end of the rope is passed back over it (whence its name) and put through the loop thus formed. It is used at the end of a rope to prevent the strands unlaying, and sometimes in the middle of a rope as a stopper knot. If the end of the rope is passed through the "bight" or loop two, three, or more times before hauling it taut, the double,

Fig. 2.—Fourfold Overhand Knot, Loose and Taut.

treble, or fourfold knot, A (Fig. 2), is obtained. This is a larger knot than Fig. 1, and is often used on the thongs of whips, being then termed a blood knot. B (Fig. 2) shows the knot hauled taut. Fig.

1 also goes by the name of the Staffordshire knot,
as it forms the insignia of the county. A Flemish
or figure-of-eight knot is shown by Fig. 3. To
make it, pass the end of the rope back, over, and

Fig. 3.—Figure-of-eight Knot.

round the standing part, and up through the first
bight. The Flemish knot is used for much the
same purposes as the preceding knots, but is
rather more ornamental.

The bight of a rope is the loop formed when a
rope is bent back on itself, in contradistinction
to the ends.

The conditions under which the ends of two
pieces of cordage have to be joined together are
various, and several methods are brought into
requisition; but it is always of considerable importance that the most suitable knot be employed
in each case. The value of some knots consists

Fig. 4.—Sailor's Knots or Reef Knots.

in the rapidity with which they can be made, of
others in the readiness with which they can be
undone; but it is an essential that the knot holds
firmly and does not slip when once hauled taut.

The commonest knot for joining the ends of two ropes, and probably the knot that is most often made, is the sailor's, true, or reef knot (Figs. 4 and 5). When correctly made it is as perfect as a

Fig. 5.—Reef Knot, Half-made.

knot can be. It can be made and undone with equal rapidity, and is very secure when taut. Its one disadvantage is that it will not answer when made with ropes of different sizes, as it then slips and comes adrift, but where the two pieces of cordage are of the same size it is most secure and reliable, the strain being equally distributed on every part. It requires a little practice to make it properly. To do this, take an end in each hand and lay one over the other, the right end being undermost; bring the left-hand end under the standing part of the right end, as shown at A (Fig. 5), and over the end at B, round it, and up through the bight at C. The key to the knot is the putting of the right end under the left when the two ends are crossed at the beginning of the

Fig. 6.—Granny or Lubber's Knot.

knot, as the left-hand end then comes naturally first over and then round the other rope, and the ends lie parallel with the standing parts, as at A (Fig. 4).

If the ends are not passed correctly, a granny, lubber's, or calf knot results. This is shown in Fig. 6. Though at first sight this seems to be a good knot, yet it is not so in reality, and when any strain comes upon it it slips and becomes useless. Fig. 7 is a granny knot, as it appears when hauled upon. It is considered a very lubberly thing to make a granny knot, and readers should practise until they can make a true knot rapidly and with certainty in any position.

The sailor's knot is invariably used for reefing sails, the ease with which it can be undone making it very valuable for this purpose. It is only necessary to take hold of the two parts on each

Fig. 7.—Granny Knot, Taut.

side just outside the knot and bring the hands together, and the loops slip over one another, as in Fig. 4, and the knot can be opened at once.

This knot has a curious peculiarity which is not generally known. If the end of one of the ropes is taken in one hand and the standing part of the same rope in the other, and both are hauled until the rope is straight, the knot becomes dislocated, so to speak, and the rope not hauled upon forms a hitch, B (Fig. 4), round the other part. This property was the secret of Hermann's celebrated trick, "the knotted handkerchiefs." After the handkerchiefs, knotted together at the corners, were returned to him by the audience, under pretence of tightening the knots still more, he treated each knot as has been described. The knots seemed firm, but really were loosened so that a touch with h s wand separated them easily.

The common bow or rosette knot is a modification of the sailor's knot. The first part of the process of making it is the same, but instead of passing one end singly over and under the other, as in the sailor's knot, both ends are bent back on themselves, and the double parts worked as before. Care must be taken to pass these doubled

Fig. 8.—Overhand Rosette Knot or Bow.

ends exactly as those described in the sailor's knot, or a granny bow will result. Some persons' shoes always come untied, the reason being that they are tied with granny instead of true bows.

Another way of joining the ends of two pieces of cordage is shown in Fig. 8. This is merely an overhand knot, made with two ropes instead of one. Sometimes it is called an openhand knot. It can be made very quickly, and there is no fear of its slipping, but if there is much strain put upon it the rope is very apt to part at the knot, in consequence of the short "nip," or turn, that it makes just as it enters the knot.

Fig. 9 shows the weaver's knot partly made, and Fig. 10 the same knot completed, but not hauled taut. Weavers call this the "thumb knot," as it is made over the thumb of the left hand, and is used by them in joining their "ends" as they break. The rapidity with which they make the knot, snip off the ends, and set the loom going again is wonderful. Netters use this knot to join their twine, and it also forms the mesh of the netting itself, though, of course, it is then made in a very different way. In making the

Fig. 9.—Weaver's Knot, Half-made.

weaver's knot, the two ends to be joined are crossed in the same way as in the sailor's knot, placing the right end under, and holding them with the thumb and finger of the left hand at the place where they cross. The standing part of the right-hand rope is then brought back over the thumb and between the two ends, as shown in Fig. 9. The end A is then bent down over it, and held with the left thumb, while the knot is completed by hauling on B.

An excellent way of joining two ropes is

illustrated by Fig. 11. The ends are laid alongside one another, overlapping each sufficiently to give room for the knot to be made. The double parts are then grasped in each hand and an overhand knot is formed, which is made taut by hauling on both parts at once, as if the knot were single.

Fig. 10.—Weaver's Knot, Closed.

Though the above is the easiest way to make the knot, it is not available where the ropes are fast. In this case a simple knot is made on the end of one rope, but not drawn taut. The end of the other rope is passed through the bight of the first, and a second loop formed with it alongside the first. The knot is closed by drawing the two ropes as before. This is in every way an excellent knot, and very secure.

Fig. 12 shows the ends of two ropes joined by means of a Flemish knot. It does not require

Fig. 11.—Overhand Knot Joining Two Ropes.

much description, and is made after the manner of the knot last described.

The fisherman's knot (Fig. 13) derives its name from the fact that it is always used for joining silkworm gut for fishing purposes. In making it, the strands are made to overlap one another, and an overhand knot is made with one end round the other strand. The strands are turned round, and

Fig. 12.—Flemish Knot Joining Two Ropes.

another overhand knot made with the other end round the first strand. When the knot is tightened

Fig. 13.—Fisherman's Knot.

by hauling on the standing parts, one knot jams against the other and holds securely. The knot is improved by putting the ends twice through their respective loops, as at A (Fig. 2, p. 15). The size of the knot is increased by this means, but it will stand a much heavier strain, so that it is advisable to do this whenever the size of the knot is not of paramount importance.

The whipcord knot (Fig. 14) is used to fasten the lash to a whip. The lash B is laid across the ends of the thong A which are turned up over it.

Fig. 14.—Whipcord Knot.

The lash is brought completely round the thong and through the loop it makes, which secures the ends of the thong firmly. If a silk lash is used, the short end is cut off, but if whipcord, the two ends are generally twisted together for a few inches, as at B, and an overhand knot made with one end round the other, to secure them. The remaining part is left somewhat longer, and another overhand knot at the end prevents it from unravelling.

CHAPTER III.

EYE KNOTS, HITCHES, AND BENDS.

ONE of the simplest eye knots is shown by Fig. 15, and is known as the "running" or "slip knot." A bight is first formed, and an overhand knot made with the ends round the standing part. The last named may be drawn through the knot, and the eye made to any size required. There is less chance of the knot coming undone if an overhand

Fig. 15.—Running Knot.

knot is made on the end A. With this knot a sailor ties his neck-handkerchief.

Fig. 16 is the "fisherman's eye knot." A bight is first made of sufficient length, and an overhand knot formed with the standing part round the other strand; the end is now passed round the standing part, and knotted as before. Thus there is a running knot A, with a check knot B, which, when hauled upon, jam tight against one another, and hold securely. This is one of the best knots for making an eye in fishing, as the strain is divided equally between the two knots.

A common way of making an eye on the end of a piece of cord is illustrated by Fig. 17. It is practically the same knot as Fig. 8 (p. 19), except

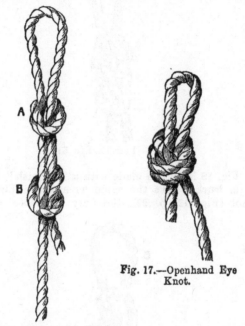

Fig. 17.—Openhand Eye Knot.

Fig. 16.—Fisherman's Eye Knot.

that only one rope is used. The end is brought back along the rope to form the eye, and an overhand knot made with the two parts. This knot, from being so easily made, is often used, but it lacks strength, like the openhand knot (Fig. 8), and should not be used where it is required to bear much strain. It will have been noticed how very often openhand knots form the component parts of other knots.

Fig. 18.—Flemish Eye Knot.

Fig. 18 is an eye made with a "Flemish" knot. It is worked just the same as a single Flemish knot (Fig. 12, p. 22), the only difference being

Fig. 19.—Crabber's Eye Knot.

that two parts are used instead of one. It is stronger, but clumsier, than the one just described, and is not much used.

The "crabber's knot" (Fig. 19) is a curious and not very well known knot, but it is unlikely to part when strained. To make it, bring the end back to form a loop, taking it first under and then over the standing part, up through the main loop, over the standing part again, and up through its own bight. Before the turns are hauled into their places, the knot will slip on the part A, as

Fig. 20.—Bowline Knot.

in an ordinary slip knot; but if the part B is hauled upon, the strand A, which passes through the centre of the knot, rises, and the coil which goes round it jams, making the knot secure: so that it may be used as a running knot or otherwise, as desired. This is also called a running knot with crossed ends.

The "bowline knot" (Fig. 20) cannot slip, and is therefore always used for slinging a man for the purpose of doing some particular piece of work:

the workman sits in the sling. The end is first laid back over the standing part, so as to form a loop; the end is then passed up through the loop, round the back of the standing part, and down through the loop again. Hauling on the end and the standing part makes the knot taut.

A modification of this knot, called a "Bowline on a Bight," is shown by Fig. 21. The loop is made as in the previous knot, only with the two

Fig. 21.—Running Bowline on Bight.

parts of a doubled rope; the bight is then passed up through the loop, opened, and turned backwards over the rest of the knot, when it appears as illustrated. To untie it, draw the bight of the rope up until it is slack enough, and bring the whole of the other parts of the knot up through it, when it will readily come adrift. If the standing parts of the rope are held fast, it puzzles the uninitiated to undo it.

A "Running Bowline" has the knot made on the end after it has been passed round the standing part, thus forming a loop through which the main rope will run. Two ropes may be joined together by making a bowline in the end of one of them, and putting the end of the other through the bight, and forming with it another bowline on its own part. This is often used to join hawsers together.

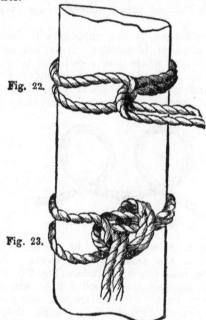

Figs. 22 and 23.—Running Knot with Two Ends, Loose and Fastened.

Fig. 22 shows a method of making a rope fast to a post or pillar. The rope is doubled and passed round the post, and the ends put through the loop. For greater security, the ends may be passed round the standing part and through the bight thus formed, as in Fig. 23; or, instead of

passing the cords through the bight, a loop may
be formed by doubling the ends, and this loop put
through the bight, thus forming a slippery hitch.
This knot has the advantage of being more readily
undone than the other one, as it is necessary
merely to pull at the ends, and the rope is released
at once. The ends may also be secured by making
a Flemish knot on them, instead of an overhand
knot.

The remainder of this chapter will discuss a
different class of fastenings. It is not easy to
state, however, where knots end and bends and
hitches begin; indeed, a tie that, in certain circumstances and made a particular way, is called a
" knot," differently constructed, and under other

Fig. 24.—Two Half Hitches.

conditions, is called a " bend " or " hitch," though
the result is the same in both cases. As an
illustration, take two half hitches (Fig. 24), which,
if made in another way round a pole, are called
a " builder's knot." If readers will analyse the
knots illustrated throughout this book, they will
find several other similar instances. A (Fig. 24)
is a single hitch, being merely a loop formed in a
rope. This is readily done by holding the rope
in the left hand, and giving it a twist with the
right; the loop then forms itself, as it were.
When a tightly laid piece of cordage is twisted,
these loops are apt to rise and form "kinks,"
which are very objectionable, as the cord is sure
to part at the kink when a strain is put on it.

It is still worse in the case of wire, which breaks readily when kinked. Tight, hard cordage should always be well stretched before it is used, to avoid kinking.

Two half hitches (Fig. 24) are a useful knot for a variety of purposes, as they are quickly made, and will not slip, no matter what strain is put upon them—indeed, the more they are hauled upon the faster they hold. They are the best means of making a rope fast to a hook. First one hitch is slipped on, and then the other on the top of it, and the rope is fast in less than two seconds. This knot is used by surgeons in reducing a dislocation of the thumb joint.

Fig. 25.—Builder's Knot, or Clove Hitch.

Fig. 25 is the builder's knot, merely two half hitches, but as it is used in places where the hitches cannot be passed over the ends of the timber it is made by holding one end in the left hand, passing the rope round the pole, under the end, round the pole again, above the first part, and under its own part; from its non-liability to slip laterally this knot is always used to fasten one pole to another in fitting up scaffolding, from which circumstance it has acquired its name. If, instead of beginning the knot as in Fig. 25, the end is passed, after it has gone round the pole, two or three times round the other part, as in Fig. 2 (p 15). the remainder of the knot is rather

more easily made, as it holds itself taut, and will
not slip while the end is put round to complete
the fastening.

A "builder's double knot" is made in the
same way, except that the end goes round again,
as before, and underneath its own part, so making
it much stronger. When a builder's knot is made
on a rope for the purpose of securing a small
line to a stout rope, it is called a "clove hitch."

The "timber hitch" (Fig. 26) is a rough and
ready way of securing a piece of timber or any-

Fig. 26.—Timber Hitch.

thing similar; it is made by bringing the end of
a rope round the timber, then round the standing
part, and then, taking two or more turns, round
its own part. The pressure of the coils one over
the other holds the timber securely, and the more
it is hauled on the tighter it holds. It can be
cast off readily.

Fig. 27 is the "killick hitch," a modification of
the timber hitch, used for fastening a stone to the
end of a rope. After making a timber hitch and
hauling it taut, a single hitch is made, and slipped

over the end of the stone alongside of it. Some of the best fishing grounds are on rocky coasts where an anchor would not hold; and if it did,

Fig. 27.—Killick Hitch.

there might be considerable risk of losing it altogether, from its jamming in the crevices of a rock. In these places a killick, or large stone, slung as shown in Fig. 27, is used, which holds

Fig. 28.—Magnus Hitch.

the boat by its own weight, without any risk of getting fast to the ground.

The "magnus hitch" (Fig 28) is a method of securing a rope to a spar, as there is but little tendency to slip endways along the spar. In making it, take the end of the rope twice round

Fig. 29.—Fisherman's Bend.

the spar, in front of the standing part, round the spar again, and then through the last bight.

The "fisherman's bend" (Fig. 29) consists of two round turns round a spar, and a half hitch round

Fig. 30.—Rolling Hitch.

the standing part, and through the turns on the spar, and another half hitch above it, round the standing part. It is used for bending studdingsail halyards to the yard, and, in yachts, for bending on the gaff topsail halliards.

A "rolling hitch" (Fig. 30) is made by taking

Fig. 31.—Topsail Halliard Bend.

three round turns round a spar, and then making two half hitches round the standing part of the rope, and hauling taut.

The "topsail halliard bend" (Fig. 31) is used

Fig. 32.—Racking Hitch.

chiefly on board yachts, and is made by bringing the rope twice round the spar, back round the standing part, under all the turns, over two turns, and under the last. This hitch is shown open for the sake of clearness, but in practice it is usual to jam the coils close together, and haul them all taut.

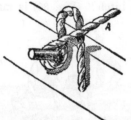

Fig. 33.—Slippery Hitch.

Fig. 32 is a "racking hitch," for hitching a rope on to the hook of a block. Two bights are made in a rope, these are turned over from the

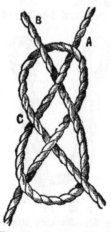

Fig. 34.—Carrick Bend.

operator two or three times, and the two loops are put on to the hook. This is sometimes called a "cat's paw."

The value of the "slippery hitch" (Fig. 33) consists in the readiness with which it can be cast off in case of emergency; at the same time, it holds securely while there is a strain on the rope A. If the mainsheet of small boats is made fast at all, always a more or less risky proceeding, a slippery hitch should always be used as a start. A sharp pull at the end of the rope lets the sheet go at once.

For the "carrick bend" (Fig. 34) lay the end of a rope over the standing part to form a loop; put the end of another rope under the bight over the standing part at A, under the end at B, over

Fig. 35.—Bending Sheet to Clew of Sail.

the rope again at C, under its own part, and over the rope B, and haul taut. The parts A and B form the first loop made. This bend generally is used for binding hawsers together, to increase their length for warping or towing. It can be undone readily without the aid of a pricker or marlinespike, which would have to be used for many knots after they had been in the water. As in the sailor's knot, it is only necessary to grasp the ropes just outside the knot, and push the loops inwards, and the knot comes adrift at once.

Fig. 35 shows the clew of a sail, and the method of bending the sheet on to it. This is termed a "sheet bend." The sheet is not, as many suppose, a part of the sail, but is a rope used in setting a sail, to keep the clew or lower corner of the sail down to its place. In making a sheet bend, the end is passed up through the clew, round the back of it, under its own part, and over the clew again.

Fig. 36.—More Secure Sheet Bend.

The end is generally stopped to the standing part with rope yarn or other small stuff. The knot thus formed is exactly the same as the weaver's knot (Fig. 10, p. 21). Fig. 36 shows a method of giving additional security to this knot. The end is passed twice round the back of the loop before putting it under its own part. This knot is very much used by fishermen in bending a line on to a loop of gut.

Another and somewhat more complicated method of bending a rope on to a loop is illustrated by Fig. 37. B is the standing part, and A the end

Fig. 37.—Bending Rope to Loop.

of the rope to be bent on a loop already formed. Pass the end down through the loop, round over its own part, and through the loop, round the back of it, and through its own bight. When hauled taut, this holds more securely than either of the other methods, but, on the other hand, takes longer to make.

The " Blackwall hitch " (Fig. 38) is a ready way of securing a rope temporarily to a hook. The method of making it is evident from the illustration. As the standing part when hauled upon jams the end against the back of the hook, it holds much more firmly than would be supposed at first sight.

Fig. 38.—Blackwall Hitch.

The "midshipman's hitch" (Fig. 39) is an old-fashioned hitch, used for attaching a tail-block to a rope. A round turn is first made over the standing part, and the end is brought up, passed twice round above the first hitch, and then passed out underneath its own part.

The "marlinespike hitch" (Fig. 40) is used for getting a purchase on the seizing stuff when serving a rope, so as to leave the turns taut. Make a bight in the seizing stuff, and bring it back over the standing part; pass the marlinespike under the standing part, and over the sides of the bight. This is practically identical with the running knot (Fig. 15, p. 24). Seizing is described on p. 96.

broken rope also takes more power than a piece of the whole unbroken rope, as the three hands taken together require.

The shackle-bend is, as will be seen, useful in securing a rope to an eye, or even hook. The method of making is very clear, from Fig. 38. As the end passes right round both parts from the one again through of the hook, a more secure method than that of the seizing will be supposed in that case.

Fig. 39.—Midshipman's Hitch.

The *Midshipman's Hitch* (Fig. 39) is good for holding on to a tense rope, or for attaching a smaller rope to a larger one. A loop is first made round the main rope, and then another

Fig. 40.—Marlinespike Hitch.

Fig. 41 is a "regulating lashing," used when the tension of a rope requires altering from time to time. Tent ropes are secured this way, as they

Fig. 41.—Regulating Lashing.

Fig. 42.—Stationer's Knot.

require easing in wet weather, and tightening in dry. For this purpose, the piece of wood A is slipped up or down the cord, the friction of the cord against the sides of the hole fixing it sufficiently.

The "stationer's knot" (Fig. 42) is handy for tying up a parcel, as it can be made rapidly, and undone with ease. Make a running noose at the end of a piece of twine, and bring it to the centre of the parcel; take the twine round the parcel again at right angles, round the noose, and making a bight slip it under, as illustrated. A pull at the end releases the knot instantly, as can be proved by experiment.

CHAPTER IV.

RING KNOTS AND ROPE SHORTENINGS.

OFTEN it is necessary to fasten a rope to a ring, and there are a variety of methods of doing this. Fig. 43, for instance, shows the end to be passed through the ring, and a bight put under the stand-

Fig. 43.—Slippery Ring Knot.

ing part; this is a ready way of temporarily fastening the painter of a boat to the ring of a pier; as in the stationer's knot (Fig. 42, p. 41), a sharp pull at the end of the rope frees the painter at once. This is an excellent fastening for many purposes. The "boat knot" (Fig. 44) is another means of mooring a small boat. It is made in the same way as a marlinespike hitch (Fig. 40, p. 40), the only difference being that a

Fig. 44.—Boat Knot.

thowl pin or other small piece of wood is put through the centre of the knot instead of a marlinespike. By withdrawing the pin the knot

Fig. 45.—Lark Boat Knot.

comes adrift of its own accord. Fig. 45 is another form of boat knot, called the "lark boat knot,"

or " double boat knot." This differs from the last
knot, inasmuch as a bight, instead of a single end
of rope, is put through the ring; a piece of wood
is used to fasten it, as in the boat knot. It is
rather the better knot of the two.

If, instead of the ends being brought down
outside the bight after it has been passed through

Fig. 46.—Lark's Head.

Fig. 47.—Lark's Head
Stoppered.

the ring, they are put through it, a " single lark's
head " (Fig. 46) is the result, and Fig. 47 shows
the same knot " stoppered." It may be made by
passing a bight through the ring, and drawing the
two parts of the rope through the bight; or where
this is not practicable by reason of one end of the
rope being fast, the end may be passed up through

the ring behind the standing part, and down through the ring and bight again. Sometimes, instead of stoppering this knot with an overhand

Fig. 48.—Lark's Head with Crossed Ends.

knot, as in Fig. 47, the end is seized to the standing part with twine.

A "lark knot" with crossed ends (Fig. 48) is

Fig. 49.—Double Lark's Head.

made in the manner above described, except that the end comes over instead of through the bight. The ends are often stoppered as in the last knot.

If the standing part is taken in one hand and the end in the other, and drawn apart. it is nothing

Fig. 50.—Treble Lark's Head.

more than a "clove hitch" or "builder's knot" (Fig. 25, p. 31) under a different name.

In the "double lark's head" (Fig. 49) a bight is first made, and the ends passed through it; the ends are then put through the ring and through the loop just made and hauled taut. Fig. 50 shows

Fig. 51.—Backhanded Sailor's Knot.

the "treble lark's head," which is not so difficult as it looks. First bring the bight of a rope up through the ring, take one of the ends, and pass it through the bight, and up through the ring,

Fig. 52.—Capstan Knot.

and then down through its own bight; do the same with the other part and the knot is formed.

In Fig. 51 is illustrated a "backhanded sailor's

Fig. 53.—Another Form of Sailor's Knot.

knot," made by passing an end through the ring round at the back of the standing part and through the ring again, and finishing with two half-hitches round the standing part. It may also be made with the end in the last turn put under the standing part and under its own part.

Fig. 52 is the "capstan knot." To make this, cross the end of the rope after it is through the ring, bring it round the standing part, through the first bight and through its own bight, thus forming a sort of figure-of-eight knot.

Another "sailor's knot," composed of two half-hitches round the standing part of the rope, is shown by Fig. 53. This is one of the most useful

Fig. 54.—Gunner's Knot.

and easily-made knots known, and is used as a mooring knot.

A "gunner's knot" (Fig. 54) is simply a "carrick bend" (Fig. 34, p. 36), made with the two ends of a rope after it has been passed through two rings. Gunners themselves call this a "delay knot."

The knot shown in Figs. 55 and 56 is called "manharness," or the "artilleryman's knot," and is used when hauling guns over a difficult country, when horses cannot be employed. It is a valuable knot where heavy weights have to be drawn with ropes, as by its use a man can exert his strength

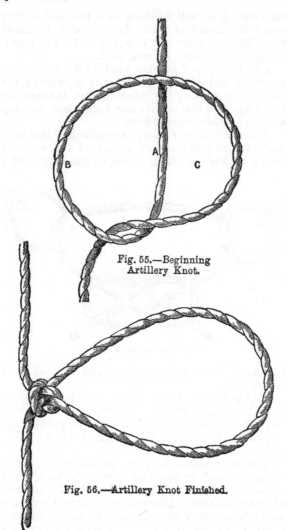

Fig. 55.—Beginning
Artillery Knot.

Fig. 56.—Artillery Knot Finished.

to much greater advantage than by merely grasping the rope with his hands. To make it, form a half-hitch, turn it round, and lay it against the standing part. This is, in fact, a marlinespike

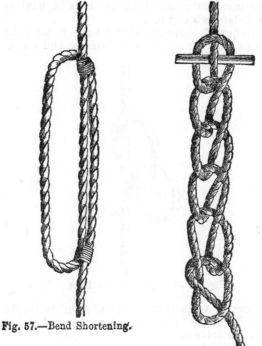

Fig. 57.—Bend Shortening.

Fig. 58.—Chain Knot.

hitch, and is represented in Fig. 40, p. 40. Now pass the right hand into the bight c, and going under A, as shown in Fig. 55, grasp the part B, and draw it through c until a loop of sufficient size is made. When using it, the head and one arm are passed through the loop illustrated in Fig. 56, which shows the knot finished. A little care is required in closing the knot, so that the turns may jam properly one against the other, or the knot will slip. When several men are employed, a bow-line is generally made at the end of the rope, and as many loops as there are men to haul at equal distances along it.

It frequently happens that a rope is too long for its purpose, and as it is inadvisable and waste-

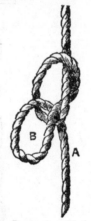

Fig. 59.—Beginning Chain Knot.

ful to cut it, some method of reducing its length has to be devised; hence have arisen what are termed "shortenings."

The "loop" or "bend" shortening (Fig. 57) is the simplest of these. The rope is merely bent as much as is required, so as to form two bights, and the two parts seized together with small stuff. This is a simple and good method of shortening ropes.

The "chain knot" (Fig. 58) is another method of shortening ropes In beginning it, make a running knot (Fig. 59), and draw a portion of the part A through the loop B; do this with the fore-finger and thumb of the left hand. It will now form another loop, through which a fresh piece of A is to be passed. This process is to be repeated until all the slack of the rope is taken up Finish it off by putting a piece of stick or a belaying-

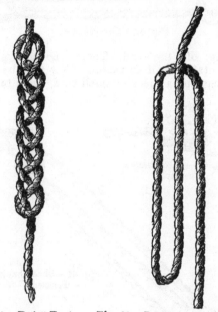

Fig. 60.—Twist Knot.   Fig. 61.—Beginning Twist Knot.

pin through the last loop, or by drawing the end itself up through the bight.

The "twist knot" (Fig. 60) is another shorten-ing. Place the cord to be shortened as in Fig. 61, bring one of the outside parts over the middle strand, and the outer strand on the opposite side is brought over this, which is now the middle part. This is continued as long as required, the outside strand alternately being placed over the centre strand, as in an ordinary three-plait. Fig. 60 shows the plait completed, and the manner of

Fig. 62.—Sheepshanks.

finishing off the end. These shortenings are ornamental as well as useful. They may be used for thickening a piece of small cord, so as to give

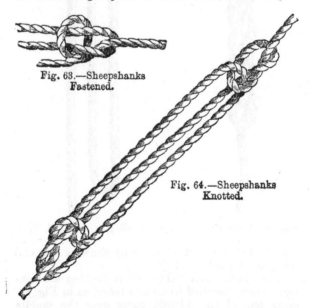

Fig. 63.—Sheepshanks
Fastened.

Fig. 64.—Sheepshanks
Knotted.

more substance where it has to be hauled upon, and thus prevent the hand being cut with the cord.
Fig. 62 is the " sheepshanks " or " dogshanks "

—a common and old-fashioned method of shortening, applicable to any size of cordage. The twist and chain knots are not suitable for very stout rope. Two bights are formed in the rope, as in Fig. 61; a half hitch is then made at each end, and slipped over the bights. This is made more secure if a seizing is put round the two parts, A, B (Fig. 62). It can also be secured when ends of

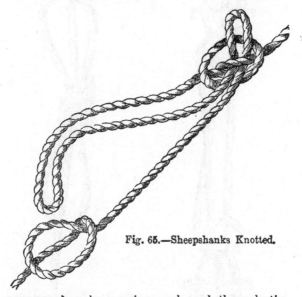

Fig. 65.—Sheepshanks Knotted.

rope are free by passing each end through the adjoining bight, as shown in Fig. 63.

Fig. 64 is a "knotted sheepshanks." It differs from the last in that the ends are fastened rather differently. The two bights are made as before, and each end, after passing through the bight nearest to it, is put through the bight it has just made, thus forming an overhand knot at each end. In making Fig. 65, the parts of the rope are arranged as before. A marlinespike hitch (Fig. 40, p. 40) is made at each end and the bight put through it. The left side of Fig. 65 shows the knot

Fig. 67.—Knot Shortening.

Fig. 66.—Boat Knot Shortening
or Sheepshanks Toggled.

made, and the bight in the act of being passed through it. It goes over the outside strand, under the centre one, and over the next. On the right side of the figure the loop is shown in its place, ready to be hauled taut.

The " boat-knot " shortening (Fig. 66) is another form of sheepshanks. The ends are secured by

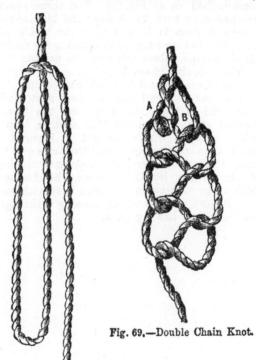

Fig. 69.—Double Chain Knot.

Fig. 68.—Beginning Knot Shortening.

bringing a portion of the loose part of the rope through the bight at each end, and toggling it with a belaying-pin or piece of wood, as in the boat knot (Fig. 44, p. 44). It is loosened readily, and can be made when both ends are fast.

The "knot" shortening (Fig. 67) is a ready mode of taking up the slack of a rope, though it is not suitable for very stout ropes, and can be made only where one end of the rope is free. The rope is laid as at Fig. 68. The three parts are grasped with both hands near the bights, and an overhand knot is formed with the whole of the strands. It forms a good shortening for moderate-sized cordage, where the strain is not too heavy.

The "double chain knot" (Fig. 69) is perhaps the most ornamental knot of this group. A turn is first taken round the standing part, and the loose end is then passed through the loop thus formed at A. In doing this another loop B is made, through which the end is brought. The end is thus continually passed from one side to the other through the preceding loop until the knot is of the proper length. It may be finished, if desired, by making an overhand knot with the end over its own part, or merely passing it through the last loop, and hauling on it.

CHAPTER V.

TIES AND LASHINGS.

A "WEDDING knot" or tie, used for fastening together the eyes at the ends of two ropes, is shown by Fig. 70. It is made by passing rope-yarn or marline through the eyes backwards and forwards

Fig. 70.—Wedding Knot.

until strong enough, and then is fastened by taking several turns round the middle and fastening the ends with a reef knot. This forms a sort of hinge between the ropes.

The "chain knot," for lashing to a spar is illustrated by Fig. 71; a clove-hitch is first formed round the spar, and as many single hitches as required are then made. It may be finished off with any secure knot. Fig. 72 shows another and better way of making the chain knot. An overhand knot

Fig. 71.—Chain Knot Lashed to Spar.

is formed at each turn, and consequently it is much more secure than Fig. 71. This is used for bending yachts' sails to the gaff. As each turn forms a knot if the cord parts, the remainder holds firm.

and does not necessarily come adrift, as it would be almost sure to do it if fastened as in Fig. 71.

Fig. 73 is a "cross lashing," employed when a lever is used to a rope. After several turns round the rope, the lashing is crossed round the

Fig. 72.—Improved Chain Knot.

lever and fastened with a reef knot. All these lashings are used when several men are required to haul on large ropes at the same time.

For the "necklace tie" (Fig. 74) several turns are taken round the spar to be joined, then two turns round the lashings, and it is secured with a reef knot. When this is used as a lashing for shearlegs, the crossing of the two legs puts a strain on the knot, and effectually secures it. For this purpose it is called a Portuguese knot.

Fig. 75 shows a "packing knot," used for securing large pieces of timber together. It is used near stone quarries for holding the blocks of stone on to the carriages by which they are moved. Fig. 75 represents a block of granite secured to a trolley with packing knots. Two or

Fig. 73.—Cross Lashing.

three turns are made somewhat loosely with cordage round the block and its carriage ; a stout piece of wood is then inserted under the coils, and twisted round until all the slack is taken out and the cordage is taut. The end of the lever is then secured with twine to the side of the carriage, as shown in the right side of the figure. The other lashing is supposed to be all ready for tautening up.

It is often necessary to lash two things together

Fig. 74.—Necklace Tie.

without showing an external knot, which would spoil the smoothness and neatness of the work—as, for instance, in whipping the two parts of a broken fishing-rod together. Fig. 76 shows a common method of finishing off whipping without showing a knot. Lay one end forward, as at A, then pass the other end round and round a sufficient number of times, hauling taut each time ; three or four loose turns are now made, and

Fig. 75.—Packing Knot.

the end passed under them backwards ; these are worked down into their places, and when the ends are hauled taut and cut off the job is completed. The end A need not come so far as shown in Fig. 76, but may be hidden under the coils.

Fig. 77 is another method of accomplishing the purpose. Instead of a single end, as in the last case, a bight of the seizing stuff is laid along the part to be whipped, and the turns passed over it; when these are completed the end is passed

Fig. 76.—Finishing off Whipping.

through the bight, as at A. The end B is now hauled upon to bring the bight and the end of the rope snug under the coils. There are now two loops interlacing at the centre of the work, and these cannot come undone. When the ends A and B are cut off close to the turns, the whole is fair and smooth.

"Nippering," or "packing," is shown in Fig. 78. This is a method of securing two ropes together with cross turns; these are hauled taut

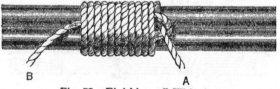

Fig. 77.—Finishing off Whipping.

jambing the ropes together, and are further secured by round turns over all, with a reef knot at the ends.

The "west country whipping" (Fig. 79) is an excellent method, and deserves to be practised

oftener than it is. Bring the middle of the
material used under the part to be whipped, raise
the ends and tie an overhand knot, lower the
ends and tie another underneath; continue tying
a single knot above and below alternately, finish-

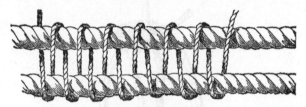

Fig. 78.—Nippering.

ing with a reef knot; or a round turn or two may
be taken and the ends may then be secured; but
a reef knot is the most usual way of fastening off
this whipping. This is not quite so neat-looking
a method as Figs. 76 and 77, but it is very strong
and trustworthy, and is an excellent way of fastening large hooks, such as those used for cod or
conger, on to a line.

A "catspaw" (Fig. 80) is used for attaching a

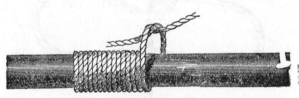

Fig. 79.—West Country Whipping.

rope to a tackle hook. Fig. 81 shows how to begin
it. A loop is made, and laid over the standing
part so as to form two bights; these are rolled
over two or three times, and the hook inserted in
them. When the standing part is hauled upon, the

others than it is. Draw the middle of the
material just under and nearer to the whipped; take
the end, and tie an ordinary knot, using the
end and the smaller [illegible]; until this
knot will have [illegible]

Fig. 80.—Catspaw.

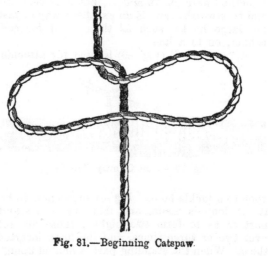

Fig. 81.—Beginning Catspaw.

hooks take the form shown in Fig. 71 (p. 59), and will not slip.

Fig. 82 shows a way of securing a block to a

Fig. 82.—Securing Block to Rope.

rope with a selvage strop. The middle of the selvage is placed against the rope, and cross turns taken until the bights come together, when the loop of the block is put through them.

CHAPTER VI.

FANCY KNOTS.

ALTHOUGH these knots are termed fancy knots, they are not necessarily used for ornamental purposes, but are often of considerable utility; indeed, they could hardly be done without aboard ship.

One of the commonest knots of this kind is the "wall knot"; Fig. 83 shows this ready for haul-

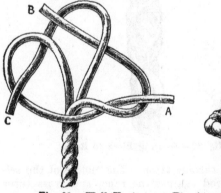

Fig. 83.—Wall Knot.   Fig. 84.—Stopper Knot.

ing taut. First unlay the strands at the end of a rope and make a bight with one strand A; hold this to the standing part with the thumb of the left hand, make a loop with the next strand B round the end of the first strand, and bring the remaining strand C round the end of the strand B and through the bight of A.

If the ends are taken round once more and

brought up in the centre of the knot, it is called
a "stopper knot" (see Fig. 84). In this case the

Fig. 85.—Beginning Crowning.

ends are whipped together and cut off level. Fig.
84 is the stopper knot finished. Fig. 85 shows
the crowning begun. Open the strands of a rope
as before, but do not put a seizing round them.

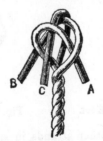

Fig. 86.—Crowning Complete.

Lay the strand A down over the centre of the
rope, and then bring B down over A and strand

c over b and through the bight of a. Fig. 86
shows how the strands tie when they are nearly
taut. The strands in Fig. 85 are hardly in the
position which they occupy when the knot is
actually being made, as they are then much
snugger.

Fig 87.—Beginning Manrope Knot.

Crowning is used by itself as a method of preventing the strands of a rope unlaying while in
use. In this case, after crowning as above, pass
one end over the next strand in the standing
part, and under the following one. Do the same

Fig. 88.—Manrope Knot.

Fig. 89.—Tack Knot.

to each of the other strands in succession. This
may be repeated and the ends cut off. Masons,
whose ropes have to stand a good deal of knock-
ing about, generally use this plan; for this reason
it is called "masons' whipping." Though very

strong and standing hard usage well, this is not
the neatest way of finishing the ends of a rope.

Crowning may also be used in connection with
other knots. For instance, it is possible to crown
first and wall afterwards, as shown in Figs. 87
and 88. Fig. 87 shows the crowning in the centre
of the knot hauled taut; this is made on the end
of a rope as just described. Now make a single

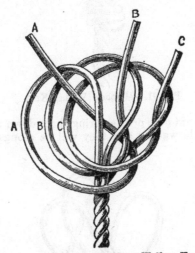

Fig. 90.—Beginning Matthew Walker Knot.

wall knot under the crowning. When the knot is
tightened it will appear as in Fig. 88, and is called
a "manrope knot." A single "wall knot" may
be crowned after it is made; a single wall and a
single crown are the result. Wall again by passing
one end under the part of the first walling next
to it and bring it up through the same bight, and
do the same with the other two strands, and the
result is a knot with a double wall and a single
crown. A double-walled double-crowned, called a

"Tack Knot," is made as the last knot—that is, double-walled and single-crowned. Now lay the ends by the sides of those in the single crown, and

Fig. 91.—Matthew Walker Knot.

with the aid of a pricker bring them down through the double walling and they will be alongside the

Fig. 92.—Beginning Diamond Knot.

standing part of the rope. The knot is shown completed, with the ends cut off, in Fig. 89.

In Fig. 90 is shown a Matthew Walker knot

open ready for being hauled taut. After putting
a seizing round the rope and unlaying the end as
before, bring one strand A round the rope and put
it through its own bight, the next strand B
underneath, through the bight of A and through
its own bight, and the last strand C underneath
through both the other bights, and lastly through
its own bight. Fig. 91 shows the knot completed.

The "diamond knot" is an ornamental knot
made some distance from the end of a rope; it is

Fig. 93.—Diamond Knot before Hauling Taut.

therefore necessary to unlay the rope considerably
more than is required for the preceding knots.
To form a diamond, bring each of the three strands
down alongside the standing part of the rope,
thus forming three bights, and hold them thus
with the left hand. Take the first strand A (Fig.
92), and, putting it over the next B, bring it up
through the bight of the third strand C. Take
the end of the second strand over the third and
up through the bight of the first. The last strand
is brought over the first and up through the bight
of the second. Haul taut and lay the rope up

again. Fig. 92 is the way the knot is begun, showing the manner of taking the first strand. Fig. 93
shows the loops in their places with the ends
through them before they are hauled taut, and
Fig. 94 shows the knot finished. Remember that,
after the bights are formed down the standing
part, each end successively goes over the strand
next to it and up through the loop beyond. This
knot is the " single diamond."

For a "double diamond" (Fig. 95) make a single
diamond as above, without laying up the strands ;

Fig. 94.—Single Diamond   Fig. 95.—Double Diamond
   Knot.   Knot.

the ends are then made to follow the lead of the
single knot through two single bights, the ends
coming out on the top of the knot. The last
strand passes through two double bights. When
the ends are hauled taut they are laid up as before.
The last four knots are used for the ends of lan-
yards, man and ridge ropes, yoke lines, etc.

The "shroud knot" (Fig. 96) is of use in joining two ropes together, particularly for joining a
stay or shroud that has been carried away. The
ends of each rope are unlaid, and placed within
one another as in splicing, the parts not unlaid
being brought closely together. Make a wall knot

(Fig. 83, p. 66) with the strands of one rope round the standing part of the other rope; turn the ropes over, and do the same with the other set of ends, and they will appear as in the figure. Open the strands, and taper and serve them over if the job is to be particularly neat. Two ropes of different sizes may be twisted in this way, and will be quite secure.

In making the "French shroud knot" unlay the ends and place the two ropes with the strands

Fig. 96.—Shroud Knot.

intermixed as before; bring one set of ends back on their own rope, and make a single wall knot with the other set of strands round the bights of the first set and the standing part. They can then be tapered and served as in an ordinary shroud knot.

For a "spritsail sheet knot," unlay the two ends of a rope and bring the two sets of strands together side by side; these have to be walled together as for a common wall knot. A bight is made with the first strand, the second is put over the first, the third over the second, the fourth over the third, the fifth over the fourth, the sixth over the fifth and through the bight of the first; they are then hauled taut. Crown it by laying two of the strands along the top of the knot and passing the other strands alternately over and under these two, and afterwards hauling them taut. It may be double-walled after crowning by putting the strands successively under the bights on the left of them and through the same bights, and the ends will then come up in the right position to be crowned again. This is done by following the

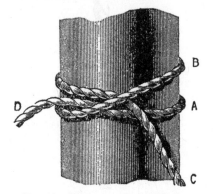

Fig. 97.—Beginning Turk's Head.

lead of the first crowning and putting the ends through the walling as before.

The "buoy rope knot" can be made on a cable-laid rope only. Unlay the main strands, and take out one of the smaller strands, of which they are composed, from each of the large strands, and then lay them up again. The small strands that have been taken out are now single and double-walled round the rope, and then laid along the divisions after the manner of weaving, and their thin ends stopped with spun-yarn A stop should be put round the rope with the spun-yarn where the knot

is to be made before it is begun, and the walling
should be right-handed.

The "Turk's Head" is a highly ornamental
knot which, instead of being made out of the rope
itself, is formed on the rope with a piece of small
stuff. A clove hitch (p. 32) is first made on the
rope (Fig. 97); this must be slack enough to allow
of the extra strands which will form part of it.
Put part A over strand B, thus twisting the two
strands; pass the end C under and up through the
bight that B now forms, then twist again by

Fig. 98.—Turk's Head.

putting B over A and run the end under and up
through the bight of A. Continue twisting the
strands by alternately putting one over the other
and at each twist bring the end under and up
through the bight which is underneath, A at the
beginning going over B; the bight which B makes
will be the under one, and therefore the one
through which the end C must be passed   The end
C must be much longer than illustrated as the
whole knot is made with this part, and as the
knot when finished contains three groups of three
strands each, it is obvious that the length of cord
used must be more than nine times the circum-

ference of the rope round which the knot is made.
Having made a sufficient number of twists (the
exact number depends on the size of the knot),
lay the end c alongside D, where it comes out of
the knot, and continue following its lead through
all its turns as it goes through the knot until the

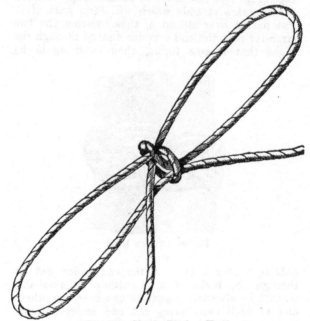

Fig. 99.—Single Pitcher Knot.

beginning is reached again. There will now be a
Turk's head of two parts. If the end is again
passed through by the side of the same strand as
before, a complete Turk's head of three parts will
be formed. Care must be taken to keep the
working strand close to and on the same side of
the strand that is being followed, or a perfect

knot cannot be formed. The first time round is the most difficult, the second is easy enough. Of course, the knot may consist of more parts if required, but three is the usual number. The ends do not require fastening in any way, as in the last round they finish in the middle of the knot under the coils, and are quite secure (see Fig. 98).

The "single pitcher" knot, known also as "Tom Fool's" knot, is shown by Fig. 99. Form two half hitches, as in Fig. 100, one lying halfway over the other. With the finger and thumb of

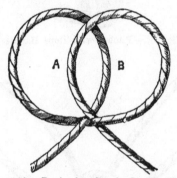

Fig. 100.—Beginning Single Pitcher Knot.

the left hand draw the part A down through the bight, and with the same fingers of the right hand bring the strand B upwards through the bight, under which it lies. Pull out the loops thus formed to a sufficient length and knot the ends together. When used to supply the place of a broken pitcher handle, the centre knot should be hauled taut, and, the pitcher being placed on it, the loops are brought up to form handles. To keep them in their places a lashing is put round the neck of the pitcher, as shown in Fig. 101. This knot is also very useful in slinging a shot when required as a weight, or for any other

Fig. 101.—Pitcher with Rope Handle.

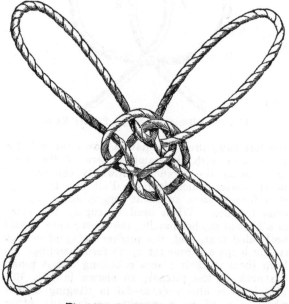

Fig. 102.—Double Pitcher Knot.

purpose. In this case the centre knot is not hauled taut but left open, forming a large loop on which the shot lies. If the ends are spliced instead of knotted a three-loop knot is made.

This knot is used also as a trick or puzzle knot, and from this arose its name of "Tom Fool's" knot.

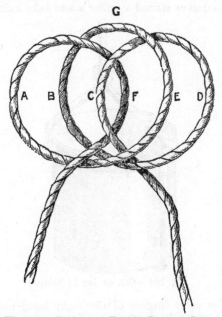

Fig. 103.—Beginning Double Pitcher Knot.

Fig. 102 is the "double pitcher" knot, which goes also by the names of "jury" knot and "true lovers'" knot. It is used as the single pitcher knot to sling a broken pitcher, but in this case there are four loops by which to carry it instead of two. In rigging a jury-mast the end of it is put through the centre of the knot before it is hauled

taut; the stays to support and steady the mast
are then made fast to the bights of the knot.
Form two half hitches in a piece of cord, as in
Fig. 103, then make another hitch, which draw behind the other hitches with the inner edge overlapping the inner edge of the first hitch, as shown
in Fig. 103. Pass the forefinger and thumb of the
left hand over strand A under B and take hold of C.

Fig. 104.—Can or Jar in Sling.

Put the same fingers of the right hand under D
over E and take hold of F. Take G between the
teeth and draw the three loops out. It is better
to make G the length required at first, as the
other loops being immediately connected with
the ends can be more readily adjusted as to size
than the upper loop. When the loops are made
the right size the loose ends are spliced together
with a short splice, thus forming the fourth loop.

Fig. 104 shows a ready way of slinging a can

to improvise a paint pot, to dip for water, etc.
Pass the end of the cord under the bottom of the
can and bring the two parts over it, and make
with them an overhand knot; open the knot, as
shown in Fig. 105, and draw the two parts down
until they come round the upper edge of the can ;
haul taut, and knot them together again over the
can, as shown in Fig. 104.

If the ends of the shamrock knot (Fig. 106)
were spliced, a four-looped knot would be formed
Though used for the same purposes as the double
pitcher knot, it is not so good as that, being more
troublesome to make and not so strong, in con-

Fig. 105.—Beginning Can Sling.

sequence of the short nip of the strands in the
centre of the knot. Fig. 107 shows the way of
making it. An overhand knot is first formed with
the ends at A; the end B is then laid across the
upper loop, brought round and under the right
loop and up through the bight C. The strand D,
after passing at the back of the upper loop, is
carried over the left loop and down through the
bight E. The loops are now adjusted for size
and the knot hauled taut. Fig. 108 gives another
way of making this knot. Two overhand knots
intersecting one another are made on the ends, as
illustrated; the part A is drawn up through the

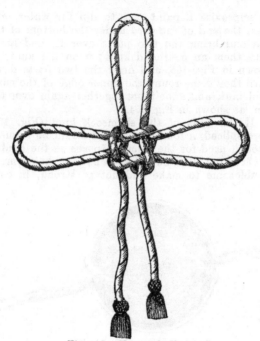

Fig. 106.—Shamrock Knot.

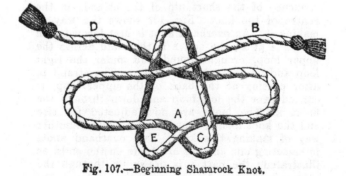

Fig. 107.—Beginning Shamrock Knot.

bight c, and the part B down through the bight D.
These form the side loops, and the top loop being
pulled out the knot is completed. By an ex-
tension of these methods knots may be made with
any number of loops, but the difficulty increases
greatly as the loops increase, so much so, that

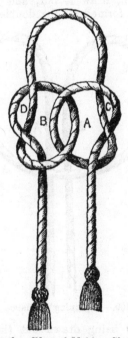

Fig. 108.—Another Way of Making Shamrock Knot.

many loops cannot be made except wire replaces
the cord.

The dalliance knot whose beginning is shown
by Fig. 109 is a trick knot difficult to learn when
it is merely seen rapidly made. The object is
to make two independent double-knots at once

on a double cord. Double the cord so that the ends
lie together; bring the bight over the standing
parts, as shown in Fig. 109, and cross the strand
A over the strand B; they will now appear as in
Fig. 110. Press the part C down between the two
strands on which it lies, and bring it up through
the opening D, draw it out, and two overhand
knots will be formed on the double cord. While

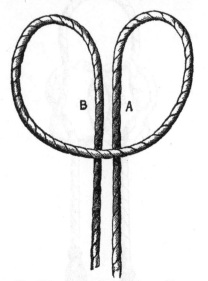

Fig. 109.—Beginning Dalliance Knot.

the part C is being drawn out through D, the
whole of the loop E must be brought up through
the bight F; this forms the upper knot. The lower
knot is made by loop F, C forming bight at top of
double cord. The finished knot is practically
the same as Fig. 16 (p. 25).

Some stage performances many years ago con-
sisted of various rope tricks. In the principal
one the performers were shut up in a cabinet,

and when the doors were thrown open they were found seated on two chairs tightly bound hand and foot. After examining the knots, the doors were closed and the men rang bells, played on the tambourine, and threw things out of a small window in the top of the cabinet. On the doors being opened again directly they were found firmly tied to their chairs as before. They were able to do this by means of an ingenious knot,

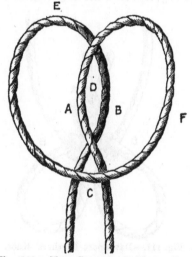

Fig. 110.—Next Stage in Dalliance Knot.

shown in Fig. 111. To perform the trick, two medium ropes each about 12 ft. long are required. First the openhand knot A (see Fig. 8, p. 19) joining the two ropes is made, the ends being passed twice through the bight to increase the size of the knot. Two running knots are made close up to this knot as at B, B. The knotted end of the rope is laid on the seat of a chair with the ropes passing down the back of the seat and under the

chair. The performer seats himself on the chair,
and, drawing the loose ends of the ropes up in front
from under it, he passes them round and round
his legs and the legs of the chair in a complicated
manner. He draws the knotted end from under
him, and, putting his arms over the back of the
chair, passes his left hand down through one loop
and his right hand up through the other. He now
turns his right hand down until the palms of both
hands are together and the fingers pointing down-

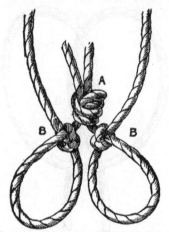

Fig. 111.—Davenport Brothers' Knot.

wards. This produces a twist in the ropes which
takes up the slack and tightens the cord round
the wrists. The large knot being between the
hands effectually hides this, and the wrists merely
appear to be as tightly bound together as they
can be. The performer has merely to reverse this
last proceeding—that is, to bring the right hand
up again, and so undo the twist—and his hand can
be withdrawn as readily as it was put into the
loop. The trick requires some practice, and the

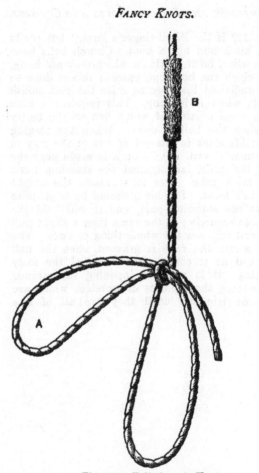

Fig. 112.—Bell-ringer's Knot.

size of the loops must be regulated by the size
of the performer's wrists. The knots should also
be so placed on the chair at the commencement
that the ropes are tight when the hands are in
the loops.

Fig. 112 is the "bell-ringer's knot," but really it is a hitch and not a knot. Church bells have a large wheel on the axle on which they are hung, round which the bell-rope passes; this is done to obtain sufficient leverage to raise the bell mouth upwards when it is rung. This requires a long rope, a good portion of which lies on the belfry floor when the bell is down. When the ringing is over this slack is hitched up out of the way in the manner shown. The loop A is made near the end of the rope, laid against the standing part, and a hitch take over it at about the height of a man's head. The hitch should be kept quite close to the standing part, and it will hold the loop quite securely; at the same time a slight pull at the end releases the whole thing at once. The part B where the rope is grasped when the bell is checked as it comes over is called the sally or tufting. It is made by opening the strands and inserting short pieces of worsted, which are afterwards trimmed until they are all of one length.

CHAPTER VII.

ROPE SPLICING.

SPLICING is a method of joining ropes by inter-
weaving together their strands. When ropes are
to run through blocks they cannot be joined by
knotting, as the knot would prevent their passing
through the block. In this case they are always
united by splicing. In driving ropes also knots
are out of the question.

For the short splice, the ends of the two ropes
are unlaid for a sufficient distance, and placed

Fig. 113.—Beginning Short Splice.

together, as in Fig. 113, the strands of one rope
going alternately between the strands of the other.
The two ropes are then jammed closely together.
The end of one rope with the strands of the other
rope is now held firmly in the left hand. Sometimes a lashing is put round the strands to keep
them down to the rope on which they lie. Pass
the middle strand A over the strand of the other
rope B which goes down to the left of it; then
bring it under C, and haul taut. Do the same to
each of the other strands in succession, putting
them over the next strand to them and under the
next beyond. Turn the rope round and do the
same to the other set of strands; this may be

repeated on both ropes. Care must be taken not to bring two strands up through one interval in the rope. Each strand should come up separately between two strands of the rope they are passed

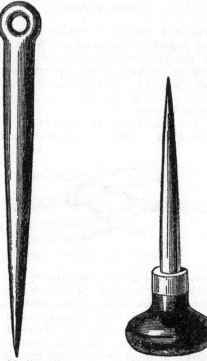

Fig. 114.—Marlinespike.   Fig. 115.—Pricker.

into. If it is desired to taper the splice for the purpose of making it neater after the ends have been interwoven, divide the yarns of which the strands are composed, pass one-half as before, and cut off the other half. To bring the rope to shape again after splicing, roll it under the foot; if small cord has been used, a piece of flat wood is substituted for the foot.

As the strands of a rope are tightly twisted together it requires some force to open a passage for the parts of one rope through the other. For this purpose, in the case of large ropes, is used a marlinespike (Fig. 114) made of iron, copper, or hard wood. Copper is preferable, as it does not rust like iron or break like wood. With small stuff a steel pricker (Fig. 115) is used. A fid is employed for very large ropes, this being merely

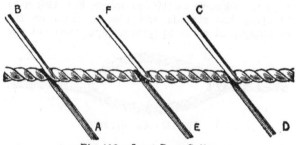

Fig. 116.—Long Rope Splice.

a tapered wooden pin generally made of lignum vitæ.

The long splice illustrated by Fig. 116 has advantages over a short one. To make it, unlay the ends of two ropes for a much greater distance than before and put the ends together. Unlay one strand A for some length, and fill up the space left by its removal with the opposite strand from the other rope, as B. Do the same with two more strands C D; C is the one unlaid, and D the one laid up in its place. Make an overhand knot with the two remaining strands E F, taking care that the ends follow the lay of the rope and not across them. Divide both strands into halves and pass one-half over the next strand, and under the following one; do this two or three times and cut all the ends off close. Work the remaining two pairs of strands the same way and the splice is finished. The rope should be well stretched before the ends of the strands are cut off.

Fig. 117 is a cut splice forming an oblong loop in the middle of a rope. The end of one rope is spliced into the standing part of another, as at A, A (Fig. 118), so as to form an eye. The end of the other rope is then spliced into the standing part of the first rope, and the spliced parts served over.

A neat way of forming an eye at the end of a rope (it is known as the eye splice, Fig. 119) is by unlaying the strands and placing them on the standing part so as to form an eye, then put one

Fig. 117.—Cut Splice.

strand under the strand next to it, and pass the next over this strand and under the second; the last strand must go through the third strand on the other side of the rope. Taper them as before by halving the strands and sticking them again.

To make a cable splice unlay the ends of the ropes to be joined for some distance, place them together and make a short splice. Leave a suitable length, and thence reduce each strand to a long taper by gradually cutting away as many yarns as necessary; neatly point over the taper and lay the ends in the intervals of the rope. Put a seizing at each end of the splice, an end seizing at the beginning of the pointing and a stop at the end of the tails. This is the best splice for cables, as it may readily be undone.

Another method of making a cable splice is to splice the ends in twice each way, then to pick out the strands, worm part of them round the cable, and taper away the rest, which should be

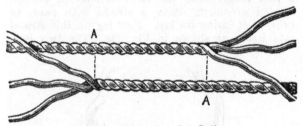

Fig. 118.—Beginning Cut Splice.

marled close down; then clap on a throat and two end seizings of ratline.

In splicing cotton ropes on the Lancashire system proceed as follows:—Short splicing the ends together is the simplest, but would not answer

Fig. 119.—Eye Splice.

for running over a small pulley or through the "swallow" of a block; in this case a long splice would suffice. If a small strop only is needed, a one-strand grommet is the neatest. A strand

from cotton rope will not keep its lay, or acquired
spiral form, and is therefore a very difficult
material to work into a grommet. Practising first
on hemp is advised. From a piece of rope about
a foot longer than the circumference of the intended grommet, unlay a strand with care, to
prevent it losing its lay. Now lay up this strand
into itself, as shown in Fig. 120. The two ends

Fig. 120.—Splicing Grommet.

will meet each other in the same crevice. Halve
these ends, and tie an overhand knot, as shown in
Fig. 121, which must not be pulled too tight, or it
will buckle-up the grommet (this will be noticed).
When this knot is quite snug down in its place,
take about one-third of the yarns out of the ends
with which the knot was made, and tuck the remaining two-thirds under two strands, missing

one (see Fig. 121, where the arrow D shows how
to tuck the end A, and arrowhead c shows
where end B will come out). Now halve these
ends, and, leaving one half, tuck the other as before; work them in nice and snug, put the grommet

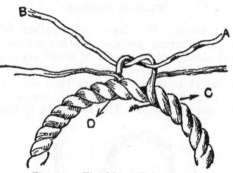

Fig. 121.—Finishing off Grommet.

on a good stretch, and trim off the ends. If the
work is well done no joint should be noticeable.
Grommets are sometimes finished off by knotting
the whole strands, then halving them, and tucking like a common splice. This is not quite as
neat, but perhaps a trifle stronger.

CHAPTER VIII.

WORKING CORDAGE.

SEIZING implies the fastening together of two ropes, or different parts of the same rope, with several closely placed coils of small rope, spunyarn, etc. The several kinds of seizings take their names from the positions they occupy in a ship's rigging. End seizing is a round seizing at the end of a rope. Throat seizing is the first

Fig. 122.—Flemish Eye.

seizing clapped on where ropes cross each other. Middle seizing is between a throat and end seizing. Eye seizing is a round seizing next to an eye in the rope.

To make a round seizing, make a small eye in the end of the seizing stuff, and, after taking a turn round both parts of the rope, reeve the ends through the eye, take two or three turns, and haul them taut with a marlinespike hitch (Fig. 40, p. 40); pass eight or ten turns close together, and heave taut. Bring the end back under these turns and out between the last two coils, and pass another series of turns on the top of the others, which are called riders, and are not hove so taut as the first turns. There is always one less of the riding turns than of the lower ones. Two cross turns sometimes are taken, passing between the ropes to be joined and across the whole of the seizing; the end is brought under the last turn, hove tight, and secured, if large, with a wall knot, crossed (Fig. 83, p. 66), and, if small, with an overhand knot, and cut off. Other seizings are done in a similar way.

Sennit is a flat rope, made by plaiting together ropeyarn or spunyarn, the outside yarns being brought over to the middle from each side alter-

Fig. 123.—Grommet.

nately. It always has an odd number of yarns, generally from five to thirteen. French sennit is braided with an even number of yarns passed over and under every other time.

Gaskets are made of braided cordage in the same manner as sennit, and are used for confining the sails when furled to the yards. They are called arm gaskets when used at the ends of the yards. Bunt gaskets are used in the middle of the yard to hold the bunt of the sail, and quarter gaskets between the middle and extremities of the yards.

A Flemish eye (Fig. 122) is a form of eye made without splicing. Unlay one strand at the end of a rope, and bring the two other strands, just as they are, against the standing part, so as to form an eye of the size required. Lay up the unlaid strand in the intervals in the rope from which it has been taken, but in the reverse way—that is, begin at the end and keep on laying it round until it comes down the standing part and lies along with the other strands. The ends are then tapered, marled down, and served over with small stuff.

An artificial eye is the end of a rope unlaid, and the yarns of which the strands are composed are separated. The yarns are now hitched round a piece of wood the size of the proposed eye. They are then marled, parcelled, and served over.

A grommet (Fig. 123) is a ring of rope made by carefully unlaying one strand from a rope and cutting it off. All the turns must be left in it.

Fig. 124.—Selvagee.

Form a ring by laying one part over the other, taking care that the turns coincide with one another. Pass one end round and round, in the lay, until all the intervals are filled up and the ring is complete. The two ends are secured as in a long splice, first with an overhand knot, and then by dividing the strands and passing half of them under the standing part, and cutting off the remainder. Grommets are used for stropping blocks, handles for chests, snorters for the heel of sprits, etc. They are very often parcelled and served to make them look neater. It is easier to make them if the rope from which the strands are taken is laid up hard.

Selvagee (Fig. 124) is a number of ropeyarns fastened together. To make it, drive two nails into a piece of board at a sufficient distance from

one another to form the size of selvagee required.
Wind ropeyarn round these to form the desired
thickness, and marl them down with spunyarn.
They are used to form a neat stropping for blocks,
or to go round a spar to which a hook is to be
fixed. Fig. 125 shows how a selvagee is employed
for fastening a block to a rope. The middle of
it is placed against the rope, and the bights passed
one over the other until they come close to the
rope, when the hook of the block is inserted.

Fig. 125.—Selvagee fastening Block to Rope.

Worming is filling the intervals between the
strands of a rope by laying spunyarn or other
small stuff into them. This renders the rope more
even and smooth for parcelling and serving. The
first end of the worming is securely stopped and
passed along one of the divisions of the rope.
When it has been carried as far as it is required,
it is stopped and laid back down another interval,
and then forward along the remaining one, and
stopped at the end. To estimate the quantity of
serving stuff required for a given length of rope,

multiply the length of rope to be served by the number of strands in the rope, and add one-third of the product. The result is the length of serving

Fig. 126.—Worming, Parcelling, and Marling.

necessary to do the work. Thus, if six fathoms of three-strand rope have to be served:— (6 × 3 = 18) (18 ÷ 3 = 6) 18 + 6 = 24. Thus 24 fathoms is the

Fig. 127.—Serving.

length of serving. Fig. 126 shows at A how worming looks when finished.

Parcelling, B (Fig. 126), is done by winding

ends of the rope pass in and around smoothly, (and a turned portion between them has been pressed and held fast in place. The reason why rope is at no period forced—the cord pushed or rolled round into its ground position in being wound up crosses over the cord as in the first is kept in strong and immediate contact with the wood in Fig. 128). This is effected by applying the rope in a slower curve round each of the ends so as to bear against, as shown in

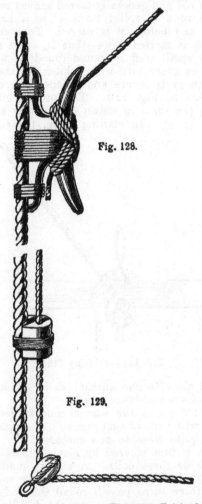

Fig. 128.

Fig. 129.

the half-hitch (beginning at the bottom, and giving it a twist for the purpose).

Fig. 129 shows the method of passing a rope between two fixed supports so that it shall run up quite steadily. Our ancestors made the part to be drawn taut by means of a ring, and by the interposition of a second (see Fig. 129). In this the rope or cord has two or three turns passed round the eye of the fixture; and then, by being led back, is attached so as to draw taut in the centre.

Fig. 128.—Belaying. Fig. 129.—Fairleader.

strips of old and generally tarred canvas smoothly
round a rope in spiral turns after it has been
wormed and before it is served. To secure the
canvas it is marled down—that is, some marline
or other small stuff is wound round it, which is
secured at every turn with a hitch, so that each
of the turns is secure and independent of each
other (see B, Fig. 126). The proper hitch for
securing the turns is shown on a larger scale in
Fig. 72, p. 60. In marling down, the coils are

Fig. 130.—Belaying Pin.

not laid close to one another as in serving, but
always at some distance apart.

Fig. 127 shows the way a rope is served or
covered with coils of spunyarn or other small stuff
laid on quite close to one another. The end of
the yarn is first secured by placing it under the
first two or three coils. A serving mallet (see
Fig. 127), after being placed against the rope, has
two or three turns passed round the body of it,
and another turn or two on the handle. This
produces sufficient friction to leave the coils taut

as the mallet is worked round the rope by its
handle. Another person is required for passing
the ball of serving stuff. The service must be put
on against the lay of the rope. A rope may be
served single-handed by carrying the serving stuff
on a large reel, with a hole in its centre large
enough for the rope to run through. This is kept
just ahead of the mallet, and the serving stuff
comes off the reel of its own accord as required.
When the mallet is within a few turns of the end,
the turns are taken off it by hand, the end is put
through them, and heaved well taut.

A rope is belayed or made fast by cross turns
round a cleat in the way shown in Fig. 128. The
cleat is assumed to be lashed to a stay or other
rope, but it is often made fast to some part of the

Fig. 131.—Toggle.

vessel. Occasionally a single hitch is put over the
upper horn of the cleat to make the rope still more
secure.

A rope is taken at right angles from one part
of a vessel to another by means of a "fairleader"
(Fig. 129). This is a block of wood with a hole in
it big enough to allow the line to run freely
through it. The back of it is grooved to fit the
rope it is lashed to. Where more than one line
has to be led, a piece of board or plank with holes
through it is used. A fairleader is not necessarily
fastened to a rope, but is fixed in any suitable
position.

A belaying pin with a rope made fast to it
(Fig. 130) is the usual way of securing running
rigging, as it can be made fast and cast off so
rapidly.

Fig. 131 shows a method of securing ropes together by means of a toggle, a piece of wood
turned to shape and having a groove in the centre,
round which the end of a rope is spliced. An eye

Fig. 132.—Another Form of Toggle.

is made in another rope by any method and the
toggle slipped into it. It is undone by slackening
the ropes and putting the toggle through the eye,
end foremost. Fig. 132 is another form of toggle,
the round piece of wood being shaped like a
button. It has a hole in the centre, through which
a rope is passed and the end knotted.

A fender (Fig. 133) protects the sides of a boat

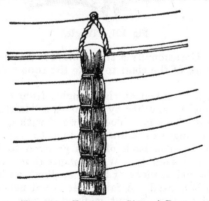

Fig. 133.—Fender on Side of Boat.

from being chafed and the paint or varnish rubbed
off. Occasionally a fender is of wood, which is
slung over the boat's side by a lanyard reeved
through a hole in the end of it, but more often it

is of canvas, stuffed with oakum and painted.
Fig 133 shows an easily made soft fender which
does not need painting. Take a piece of Manilla
rope double the length of the fender; unlay it,
open the strands, and comb them down until all
the yarns lie straight; double it and clap an eye-
seizing on it, marling it down as illustrated. A
lanyard of small cords, such as log-line, is then
spliced into the eye.

Fig. 134 shows a handsomer form of boat's
fender. This is made of a centre or "heart" of
ropeyarn worked over or grafted with short pieces

Fig. 134.—Fender with Ropeyarn Heart.

of ropeyarn called "knittles" or "nettles"; this
is a kind of weaving. The nettles are first cut to
the right length, and the middle part slightly
twisted. They are then brought snugly round a
thimble, and a seizing put under it. The heart
is put into its place and the nettles laid evenly
over it. Half of the nettles, taken alternately,
are turned back over the eye, the rest lying down
the heart. Pass a turn or two of twine or marline,
called the warp or filling, round the fender where
the nettles separate, and hitch it. The turned
back nettles must now be brought down, and those
that are down turned up over the eye. The warp

is now passed again, and hitched as before. This must be repeated until the whole of the fender is covered with a sort of woven coat as shown in Fig. 134. The ends of the nettles are brought

Figs. 135 and 136.—Thimble.

round the last turn of the warp, and interlaced in the grafting. This fender requires a lanyard the same as the last one.

A thimble, shown in side view and section by Figs. 135 and 136, is an iron ring, usually galvanised, and a rope or strop fits snugly in its flanged rim. It may be heart-shaped or round, and is used as a small eye on the end of a rope to receive another rope.

Fig. 137.—Mousing a Hook.

Fig. 137 shows a method of "mousing a hook," that is, preventing a chain slipping off a hook. A few turns of ropeyarn are passed round the end of the hook and the standing part, and the ends brought round the middle a few times, and fastened with a reef-knot.

For "stropping a block" (Fig. 138) a grommet is neat, and a selvagee still neater, especially when leather-covered. The block is first fixed in one bight, so that the lower part of the block sits on the splice, if there is one. A thimble is put into the other bight, and a seizing put on between the block and the thimble, each turn of which is hove taut with a heaver. The turns are, lastly, crossed, and the ends knotted. Fig. 138 shows the work finished. Sometimes the stropping is made

Fig. 138.—Stropping a Block.

by splicing the ends of a suitable length of rope together.

Pointing a rope is done partly to prevent it from untwisting, and partly to make it go more readily through a block or hole. Fig. 139 shows one method. The rope is unlaid for the necessary length, the strands reduced gradually, and then laid up again. The ends are finally whipped with small twine. If necessary the end is stiffened by inserting a piece of stick. Sometimes a "becket" —that is, a piece of small line with an eye at the end—is put into the end and whipped over to secure it, as in Fig. 139. Fig. 140 gives a more elaborate method. The rope is first unlaid, and a stop put on it where the unlaid part begins. As many yarns as are required are taken out and made into nettles by twisting together the two halves of different yarns. The remainder of the yarns is scraped down taper with a knife. Half of the nettles is turned back on the standing part of the rope, and the other half allowed to lie on the

Fig. 140.

Fig. 139.

Figs. 139 and 140.—Pointing a Rope.

scraped part. Two or three turns of twine are hitched round the division of the two sets of strands, and the nettles laid backwards and forwards, the weft being passed each time, as described in making the fender (Fig. 134). The end usually is whipped and a seizing put on the upper part, which is snaked, as illustrated, by passing twine diagonally under and over the outer turns of the seizing alternately—that is, if it comes

out over the upper turn, it will go under the
bottom one, under the top, and so on until it is
finished.

Fig. 141 is part of a mainstay. An eye is first
made in the end, and a mouse the shape of a pear
raised on the rope with spunyarn. Each turn
of the yarn is hove well taut with a large serving
mallet, and beaten close The eye and the rope
as far as the mouse are wormed, parcelled, and
served over; the mouse and the part below it
(the tail) are parcelled with worn canvas, well
tarred, and pointed over or grafted with small

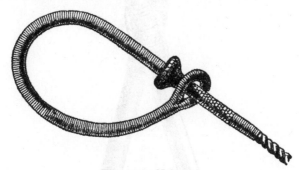

Fig. 141.—Mainstay.

stuff. The mouse is covered with nettles, and
their number diminished as they are worked into
the smaller parts. Below the pointing it is again
served over.

Shear-legs are fastened together as indicated
in Fig. 142. They are first laid side by side, and
a lashing of rope put round them. The ends of
the lashing are carried one up and the other down
to form a cross-lashing, and are knotted in the
middle. This is called a Portuguese knot. When
the legs are separated, the knot becomes very
secure.

A neat pair of yoke lines is made and fitted in

the following manner. The length of the lines
depends upon the distance of the yoke from the
after seat; that distance added to 3 ft. will give a
good length for each line Supposing the top of
the back-board to be 3 ft. from the yoke, two-and-
a-half fathoms of white cotton rope will be
necessary, the extra half fathom being allowed for
knotting, etc. Cut this in two equal lengths;

Fig. 142.—Shear-legs.

take one of these and "stop" with a few turns
of twine at 14 in. from one end and 6 in. from the
other, which will leave 70 in. between the stops
or whippings. Now unlay the longer end and whip
each strand close to the end, leaving a few inches
of spare twine on each, which will be useful when
finishing the manrope knot.

Holding the line in the left hand, make a single
wall knot, as shown in Fig. 143. The strand A
is first placed and held in position by the thumb;

B is next taken and passed round the end of A, then C round the end of B, and up through the loop formed in the first instance with A. Now

Fig. 143.—Wall Knot.

pull together evenly, but not too tightly, and with the three ends remaining work a crown (see Fig. 144), where A is crossed over the knot, then B over A, and C over B, and down through the loop formed by A. After pulling this crown together

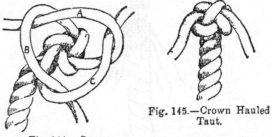

Fig. 144.—Crown.

Fig. 145.—Crown Hauled Taut.

evenly, the state shown by Fig. 145 is reached; notice that the ends lie snug against the strands of the wall knot first formed. Keeping each end on the same side of its partner, let it follow the same round, using a steel pricker to open the way between the strands. The twine ends before-

Fig. 146.—Manrope Knot.

mentioned will now be found useful in coaxing these ends through their holes. When each end has followed its partner round the wall and crown, the ends which will come out at the neck of the knot may be cut off and the manrope knot (Fig.

Fig. 147.—Pointing End of Yoke Line.

146) will be completed. A red leather washer with serrated edge is usually pushed up to the knot as a finish.

The other end of the line should be pointed.
To do this, unlay and fray out the 6 in. of end,
then pick out the yarns nearest the edge—that is,
next the whipping—and make a number of 2-ply
nettles by laying up these outer yarns, scraping
them a little with a knife to make them taper
slightly. There must be an even number of nettles,
and sufficient to lay close together all round the
"heart," which is formed by scraping away the
centre yarns to an even taper, then marling down
tight with twine as seen at D (Fig. 147). Half the
nettles must now be placed along the heart, and

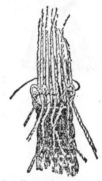

Fig. 148.—Fastening off Yoke Line.

half and half back over the whipping, picking
them out alternately. An indiarubber band is convenient to keep them in place while passing the
"warp"—that is, two turns of twine hitched
round the heart and those nettles lying along it.

The nettles must now change places; all that
were placed back must go forward, and all that
were along the heart must go back over the
whipping, and the warp is again passed twice
round and hitched; this process is continued till
the point reaches the length of 2 in., or what-
ever length of point is required. Four times the

Fig. 149.

Fig. 150.

Fig. 151.

Fig. 149.—Yoke Line Complete.
Fig. 150.—Stern Ladder.
Fig. 151.—Round of Stern Ladder.

diameter of the rope is a good rule for this. To
fasten off, all the nettles are stroked down towards
the tapered end, and all those round which the
warp was last passed are doubled back as shown
in Fig. 148, three hitched turns of the warp being
passed through all the "bites" or loops of the
nettles, which are then pulled down and cut off
with the other nettle ends. The twine stop is then

Fig. 152.—Single Rope Ladder with Chocks.

taken off and a neat snake whipping put on in its
place.

A bunting fringe is generally added as a finish,
and this is very easily made by fraying out a piece
of blue or red bunting 4 in. square, and laying the
threads down together ends even, then placing
enough of these round the yoke line to encircle it
at about 1 in. from the snake whipping. Pass a
number of turns of twine round all near the centre

of the bunting threads to form a little knob, then stroke all the bunting threads towards the point and put round all a neat snake-thread whipping just below the knob. This will form a little tassel, as shown in Fig. 149, which represents one yoke line completed. The other is, of course, made in the same manner.

A rope ladder, owing to its portability, is for some purposes more suitable than one made of wood, especially where the ladder is to be hauled up when not in use. Fig. 150 shows a rope ladder which is made of four-strand rope; the rounds are turned out of oak to the form shown in Fig. 151. The groove at the ends is for the reception of the

Fig. 153.—Toe Chock for Rope Ladder.

strands of the rope. The rounds are rather more than 1 in. in diameter, and are placed 11 in. apart. The strands are opened with a marlinespike and the rounds inserted between them, two on each side ; a seizing is put on below each round ; a round thimble is put into the upper bight, and an eye seizing is clapped on below it. The lower ends are generally spliced together, or a thimble may be spliced in, as at the upper end, if it is intended to make the lower end fast.

Another form of rope ladder is shown in Fig 152. A number of oak chocks (Fig. 153) are turned, usually about 5 in. in diameter and 5 in. deep, bored to 1 in. diameter with the grain of the wood ; this will take a 3-in. four-stranded rope. Splice an eye at one end and seize in a thimble for the lashing; put on one of the wooden steps, flat side

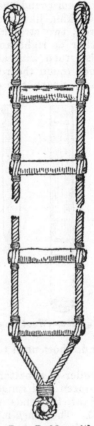

Fig. 154.—Rope Ladder with Rungs.

uppermost towards the thimble and about **30 in.** down. Insert a strand of ratline stuff between two strands of the rope, and with the two ends of the strand work a "wall knot" round the rope, then a "crown," which will bring the ends down to the first turns of the wall. Pull the parts up tight, and follow them round once; the result will be a neat knot looking like a two-parted Turk's head. If preferred, two strands may be inserted crossing each other at right angles between the four rope strands; then with all four ends work a double wall knot round the rope. Between the knots, spaced 15 in. apart, slip on the wood. Do

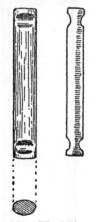

Fig. 155.—Wood Rung.

not cut off the ends short until the knots have got well jammed up.

For a 25-ft. ladder of a better kind, illustrated in Fig. 154, two dozen oval rungs of wood will be required, having at the ends scores rasped as shown at Fig. 155. The rungs may be 12 in. long. Nine fathoms of 4-in. four-stranded rope must be well stretched and the turns taken out, stretched again, etc. Middle it and seize a thimble in the bight, making this fast to a post. Then stretch out both parts together, and mark off the positions for the rungs with chalk, 12 in. apart. At every chalk mark, and round each part of rope separately, put a seven-turn whipping of tarred nettle stuff (this is sold in hanks). Now begin at the end nearest the bight or lower end, open the strands

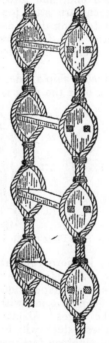

Fig. 156.—Pilot Ladder.

with a fid and spike above the seizings or whippings, and push in a rung, taking care to avoid twisting the rope by inserting the spike between the two strands best situated. When all the rungs are in and the ladder hangs without much twist, the open parts of the strands may be drawn together with a marlinespike and a piece of sennit or by carefully using a screw cramp above the rungs; then a six-turn seizing of nettle stuff put tightly on above each of the rungs keeps them in place. The top rung should be rather stouter than the rest to allow a deeper score. Splice a thimble into each end, and into each thimble a fathom of eighteen-yarn stuff for lashings. This is a good ladder to hang down clear, and is used over ships' sterns and from lower booms, the lower thimble being convenient for boats' "painters."

To hang against a ship's side, where room for the toe projecting over the rung is needed, a pilot

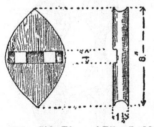

Fig. 157.—Side Piece of Pilot Ladder.

ladder (Fig. 156) is more comfortable, but more difficult to make. The steps are usually of teak, mortised into diamond-shaped side pieces (see Fig. 157) about 8 in. deep by 5 in., with a score rasped out all round the edges. About twenty-three or twenty-four of these steps will be required for a 25-ft. ladder, and eighteen fathoms of 2½-in. three-stranded rope. Prepare by stretching well as before; cut in two equal parts and mark the middle of each length. Place one of the steps immediately over the marks and seize it tight in place by bringing the parts of rope round the score on each side to meet above. If the next step is placed on this seizing and so on, the completed ladder is too stiff to roll up; it is therefore necessary to put two seizings between each step, leaving about 2½ in. of free rope between them. When the steps are thus seized in place, the ends on each side are made even, spliced together, and fitted with thimbles for the lashings.

Mats are used on board ship to prevent chafing. In making wrought mats a piece of small cord is stretched tight horizontally at about the height of a man, and fastened at each end. Across this, hanging by their middles, nettles are placed. These are often made of "foxes"—that is, three or more rope-yarns twisted together by hand, and each rubbed down with tarred canvas or a

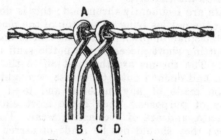

Fig. 158.—Beginning Mat.

handful of rope-yarn. Beginning with the nettle nearest the left hand, it is crossed as A (Fig. 158). Another nettle is then brought up close to the first, and crossed in the same way. The end B is then passed over the strand C, and pushed to the back; another nettle is then brought forward, crossed as before, and one part of it put over the part D, and pressed back. The work is continued this way, working diagonally until a sufficient width is obtained (Fig. 159); then, as no more nettles are added, and the outside nettle on the right is brought over from time to time, a selvage is formed as on the left side. Take care not to twist each of the nettles together at the bottom, so that they

may retain their twist until the next in succession
is brought down to interweave with them. There
is a little difficulty at starting, but afterwards
everything goes on easily. Each nettle from the
right passes over the next one to it on the left,
and is pushed back, the one that has been passed
over being taken up first over the next and pushed
back as before. Each twist should be pressed
tight as it is made. When the mat is deep enough,
a selvage is made by straining another piece of
cord along the bottom, securing both ends. As
each nettle comes down it is half hitched to this,
and the next nettle is laid up at the back of it,
and so on alternately.

Mats are frequently thrummed; this is done by
raising the nettles lying on the top of the mat with
a marlinespike or pricker after the mat is finished,
and putting short pieces of the nettle stuff underneath. The thrums are then cut off to the same
length, and opened out. Of course, wrought mats
may be made of any material and used for a
variety of purposes. They make most excellent
door-mats, and are of everlasting wear. For this
purpose they should not be made of tarred stuff.
Very pretty mats may be constructed of twine for
the foundation and various coloured pieces of
worsted for the thrums.

A kind of mat used aboard ship is called a
sword mat. It is woven, but a loom is not used.
Two small cords, or, better still, two small rods,
are secured horizontally and the nettle stuff
wound round them, the coils being laid close together. A piece of wood called a "fiddle," as long
as the width of the mat and about 2 in. wide and
$\frac{3}{8}$ in. thick, has half as many holes bored near the
lower edge as these nettles in the mat. Every
alternate nettle is secured to this by some twine
laced through the holes   Another fiddle is
fastened in like manner to the remaining nettles.
The work can now be begun. The first fiddle is

raised, and the first set of nettles consequently raised with it. What weavers call a "shed" is thus formed—that is, an opening between the two sets of nettles—and along it the weft or filling is passed by means of a netting-needle (see p. 125). The filling is driven well home with a flat piece of wood, tapered towards the edge, called a "sword." The first set of nettles is now allowed to drop, and the second set drawn up with the other fiddle. The filling is passed again and driven home as

Fig. 159.—Mat Making.

before. The work is thus continued until there is no longer room to use the sword, when the filling must be worked home with a pricker. When the mat is long enough, the filling is fastened off, and the mat is complete. These mats may be thrummed in the same manner as the wrought mats.

A softer kind of mat is made on a foundation of canvas or duck, which is very suitable for the stern-sheets of a boat or any other similar purpose. The material is cut to the right size and folded a short distance from the edge. A hole is made near the selvage with a pricker and a thrum inserted; another hole is then made a short distance from the first and another thrum put in, and so on until the row is completed. Row after row is thus worked until the mat is finished. Of course the holes, and consequently the thrums, go through both parts of the material. When the canvas is pulled straight after each row is finished, the thrums are held securely without any other fastening.

When a pattern is to be worked on the mat, the design must first be drawn on the material in pencil and the canvas folded accordingly; every fold produces two rows of thrums. White duck thrummed with pieces of cotton rope makes very nice, clean-looking mats for boat use, and as they wash well they can always be kept in good order. These mats, with a stout canvas or sacking foundation, thrummed with pieces of untarred hemp rope, serve very well for door-mats, though, of course, they will not last as long as wrought mats.

Very ornamental mats are made somewhat after the same manner as those just described. Any suitable material, of any colour, can be used for the foundation, on which the pattern must be drawn. The mat is folded along the line intended to be worked, and a common pencil laid along the ridge of the fold. The worsted or other material used is threaded in a large needle, and worked over and over the pencil, thus forming, when the pencil is withdrawn, a series of loops on the foundation. Any pattern can thus be worked, provided always that it consists of straight lines. It might be possible to form curved lines by working the loops over the first finger of the left hand, moving the finger after each loop.

CHAPTER IX.

HAMMOCK MAKING.

THIS chapter will describe the netting and slinging of hammocks.

Hammock making requires a netting needle of one of the shapes shown by Figs. 160 and 161. It

Fig. 160.—Netting Needle.

may be made from a piece of $\frac{3}{16}$-in. pearwood, beech, or boxwood about 8 in. long by $\frac{3}{4}$ in. wide. In needles as shown by Fig. 161 the cord is wound round as when filling an ordinary shuttle, and for

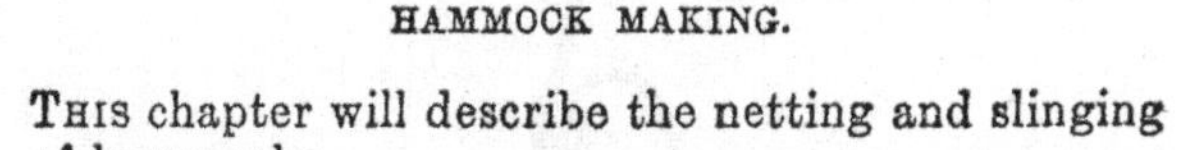

Fig. 161.—Netting Needle.

Fig. 160 the cord is brought round the end at A up one side, round the pin at B, and back the same side, the process being repeated on the other side of the needle

Fig. 162.    Fig. 163.

Figs. 162 and 163.—Mesh Stick.

A mesh stick (Fig. 162) is made of hardwood or bone about 5 in. long and of an oval shape (Fig. 163); it may be about $\frac{3}{4}$ in. by $\frac{1}{4}$ in. in section. At one end of the string to be used for the net tie a loop A (Fig. 164), and place the knot on a

nail or hook fixed in some convenient position, as
at A (Fig. 165). Place the mesh stick under the
loop as at B, put the cord under it, then pass the
needle through the loop and pull the cord tight.

Fig. 164.—Loop in Meshing.

Now place the thumb of the left hand on the cord
beyond the loop as at A (Fig. 166), and with a
turn of the wrist of the right hand throw the cord
to the position shown at B, then pass the needle
under the loop C, then through the bight of B, and
down as at D, and draw the knot tight, which

Fig. 165.—First Stage in Meshing.

should then assume the shape shown by Fig. 167.
The cord must be held firmly with the thumb at A
(Fig. 166) when pulling up the knots, as on this
depends the uniformity of the meshes.

To continue the netting the stick is withdrawn
and placed under A (Fig. 167), and the needle is
then passed under the stick as in Fig. 165, and
brought through the loop B (Fig. 167), and the
process shown by Fig. 166 is repeated to form
another mesh, this being continued to make a
chain of meshes, say forty-five or fifty (Fig. 168),
sufficient for the width of the hammock. The loop
A (Figs. 164, 165, and 168) that was first tied is
then untied, and it will then be found that all the
meshes are equal in size.

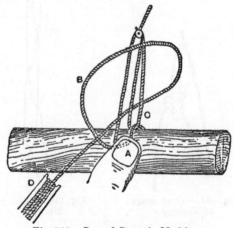

Fig. 166.—Second Stage in Meshing.

Next the chain is opened out at right angles to
the line in which it was made, as shown by Fig.
169, and working across is begun by making a
mesh at A (Fig. 169), then at B, C, and so on,
until the length of the first lot of meshes has been
reached, when the net is turned over and another
row of meshes worked until the one under A has
been reached ; then the net is turned again and
another row worked, and so on.

The meshes are worked as shown by Fig. 166, but at first, to ensure uniformity, it will be well to put the loops D, E, F, and G (Fig. 169) separately on the hook or nail as the meshes under them are made, but after a little practice a cord may be reeved through the top line of meshes, tied into a loop, and passed over the knee and then over the foot, as the work progresses.

There are three ways of forming the ends.

Fig. 167.—Third Stage of Meshing.

Fig. 168.—Chain of Meshes.

An ash stick may be used at each end to which the end meshes are looped and tied, and a piece of codline may be passed through the side meshes on each side and attached to the ends of the sticks. At each end a stout cord is secured to the stick in the form of a triangle for hanging the hammock. The second plan is to tie a number of cords together by doubling them in the centre and forming a loop, and each of the free ends, known as "nettles," is attached to one of the meshes of the net. The third and perhaps the

best plan is to reeve a cord about the size of a
little finger through the end meshes and splice it
into the form of a grommet as shown by Fig. 170.
A thimble A is fixed in the end to which the

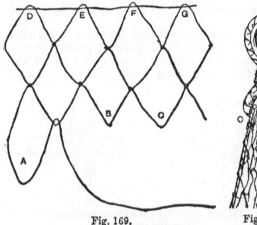

Fig. 169.

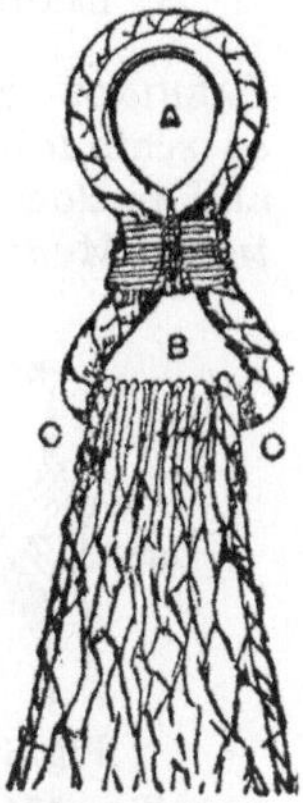

Fig. 170.

Fig. 169.—Beginning of Cross Netting.   Fig. 170.—
Hammock Clew.

supporting cords are attached, and the cords which
are reeved through the side meshes are spliced
into the eye B at c. When these "clews" are used
the net must be longer than for the sticks or
nettles.

CHAPTER X.

LASHINGS AND TIES FOR SCAFFOLDING.

LASHINGS are seizings of rope for heavy work, such as scaffolding; and the lashing of poles, ledgers, and putlogs may be now considered with advantage. Heavy scaffolding is best lashed with chain;

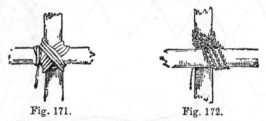

Fig. 171.   Fig. 172.

Figs. 171 and 172.—Rope and Chain Lashings for Poles and Ledgers.

and it should be noted that, while a rope lashing is hove taut by the steady strain of a heaving bar, a chain requires different treatment, and must be jerked tight with little tugs—an action similar to

Fig. 173.—Rope Lashing for Putlogs.

that used when shaking out a mat—assisted by an occasional rap with the heaver.

The rope used for lashing all parts of scaffolding should be fairly new, sound, and in size not more than 1½ in. The average length required will be about six yards, and it must be so put on that each turn of the lashing takes its share in the support. To this end the tackle supporting the ledger must not be released until the lashing is completed, otherwise the first turns will be subjected to undue strain.

Fig. 171 shows the lashing of a ledger to a pole; if chain is used a different method is necessary, and it is lashed as in Fig. 172.

Putlogs should be square, or at any rate flat on the upper and lower sides, to prevent any chance of rolling, one end being squared down in size to enter the building in the place of a header brick, the other end being lashed down to the ledger as in Fig. 173. The planks forming the stage are not lashed to the putlogs, and there is great danger in allowing them to project at one or both ends.

Poles are generally about 30 ft. long, and for high buildings it is necessary to lengthen them by lashing on an extra pole. The safest plan is to lash a half pole to the lower part of the first erected; this resting on the ground will form a footing, upon the upper end of which the lengthening pole will stand, being kept in position by three plain lashings (see Fig. 174). Should the lengthening pole be only light, and a footing not be considered necessary, a chain racking should be put on besides two rope lashings.

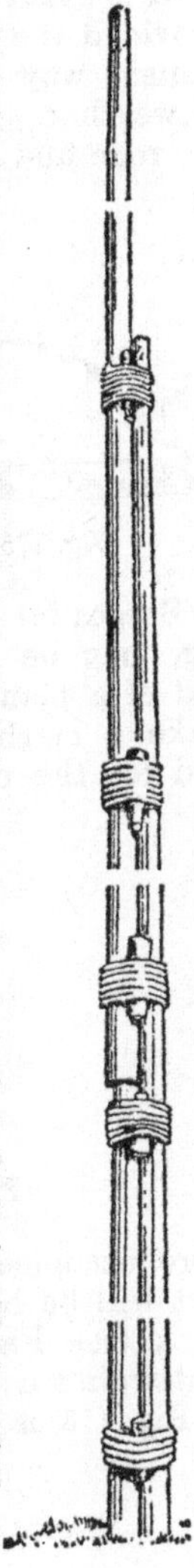

Fig. 174.—Poles Lashed and Wedged, with Footing.

It is usual to wedge scaffold lashings tight, and, provided the wedges are well shaped, it is a convenient way of tightening the work after change of weather. Badly-shaped wedges are apt to cut the rope and sometimes work out.

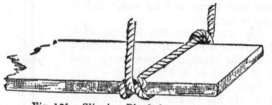

Fig. 175.—Slinging Plank for use as Stage.

Stages for painting, or small repairs on a building, may be quickly rigged up by slinging each end of a plank on the bight of a rope. For this make a marlinespike hitch (see Fig. 40, p. 40), and let the end of the plank take the position

Fig. 176.—Boatswain's Chair.

there occupied by the marlinespike; the double part will be below and the single part above the plank (see Fig. 175). For single-handed work a boatswain's chair, of which an illustration is given by Fig. 176, is convenient.

CHAPTER XI.

SPLICING AND SOCKETING WIRE ROPES.

WIRE ropes are now used to such an extent, and in such a variety of ways, that a knowledge of the best methods of handling them cannot fail to be useful to the many thousands who are brought in daily contact with them. An endeavour will here be made to give such clear and simple instructions as will enable readers, with practice, to execute any job in connection with the splicing of wire ropes. The uses that wire ropes are now put to, and the ways and occupations they are employed in, are so various, that it is almost a necessity for a man to be engaged in their manufacture to have a thorough knowledge of the different methods of handling them. For instance, it would be just as consistent to expect a sailor, used only to eye-splicing, to go to a colliery and put a long splice into a rope, to withstand the enormous stress there applied, as it would be to expect a colliery man to go aboard ship to splice the mainbrace, or any other brace.

Now Fig. 177 is a sketch-plan of an endless band rope, such as may be seen at many collieries in Great Britain. A is the driving sheave on the engine at bank, round which the rope passes three or four times, and leads off to the overhead pulley B. Then it goes down the shaft, perhaps a very considerable distance, under the pulley C, and so on to D, whence it passes round the tightening sheave E, which is movable and contrived with weights to keep the rope always tight, and so prevent surging round the pulleys and sheaves and consequent loss of power. The rope then passes

round D' to the sheave F, the driving of which is
the object aimed at, since that sheave in turn may
work either one or two hauling ropes, as at G and
H, working into the interior of the pit, in addition,
perhaps, to a pump. The load on this rope may
amount to several tons, and such a rope will therefore require a splice from 60 ft. to 100 ft. long.

Further, no matter what kind of a splice it may
be, it must be made well. If it is a ship's hawser,
at times the safety of the vessel and all it contains may depend on a splice. Again, an awful
disaster might be the result if the splice in a crane
rope were to draw.

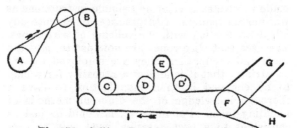

Fig. 177.—Colliery Band Rope Driving System.

There are three kinds of wire rope splices, the
short splice, eye splice, and long splice.

A short splice is a bulky splice, and is used only
for block straps, slings, etc. It is not suitable for
driving ropes or for running tackle, and should
never be put into a crane or hoist rope. It is
made by unlaying the two ends of the rope to a
sufficient length, from 1 ft. to 2 ft., according to
size, and interlaying them together as in Fig. 178.
Draw them close, and tuck the strands of one
under the strands of the other several times. It
is only a case of " over and under " as in splicing
a hemp rope. After the ends have been tucked a
sufficient number of times, about twice, each
strand will stand in most cases. Hammer all down
snug, and either cut off the ends with a hammer

and chisel or twist the wires off one or two at a time, which makes a much neater job.

An eye splice may be made in two different ways—namely, left-handed, or "over and under," and right-handed.

Left-handed splicing is undoubtedly stronger, tuck for tuck, than the right-handed method, for the "bite" on the strands is greater and the frictional adhesion is more acute. The strands and ends are practically plaited, and consequently locked together, and, no matter how the rope unlays itself, the splice is immovable. A splice like

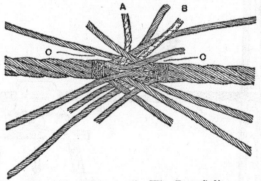

Fig. 178.—"Marrying" a Wire Rope Splice.

this should be put into every crane rope, for frequently the load when lifted from the ground spins round and unlays the rope to a certain extent.

In right-handed splicing, the ends to be tucked are simply laid several times round one strand each, and offer no resistance to any such unlaying process. However, a right-handed splice is easier and neater to make, and these splices are becoming general, some splicers making it a rule to put a "lock" in by tucking the ends once left-handed. A right-handed splice is strong enough for most ordinary purposes, but if a left-handed splice is tucked three times and put on a testing machine, it would break the rope before it would draw out; whereas, if a right-handed splice were tucked three times and put to the same test, it would pull out. However, if the right-handed splice, instead of being tucked three times were tucked eight times, it would stand any stress that could be put on it; in fact, six times through is quite sufficient for ordinary purposes.

The following is the method of right-handed

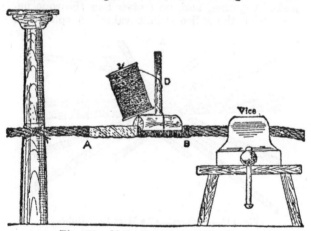

Fig. 179.—Method of Serving Wire Rope.

splicing. First fasten up the rope end from the vice to any convenient column or hook, and mark off from the end, as at A (Fig. 179), the length for the splice, which will be from 1½ ft. to 6 ft., according to the size of rope; say 2 ft. of end for 2 in. cir. rope. Measure with a string round the groove of the thimble, and transfer the length to the rope, marking it as at A B. To put a seizing on the "neck" of the splice, as in Fig. 180, add 6 in. or 8 in. to the length of rope to be served. Now take a narrow strip of parcelling—that is,

thin bagging—and bind it neatly round the rope
from A to B (Fig. 179). The rule is: Worm and
parcel with the lay, but serve the rope the other
way. Next take a serving-mallet D (Fig. 179), with
a bobbin full of spunyarn upon it, and, beginning
at B, serve over the parcelling to A. Cut off and
make fast the end of spunyarn, when the work
will be ready for turning in the thimble. A chalk
mark midway between A and B will serve as a

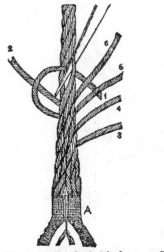

Fig. 180.—Partly-finished   Fig. 181.—Wire Rope ready
        Splice.   for Splicing.

guide in getting in the thimble straight. Next
bring the end of the rope round on the double to
form a loop, with A and B exactly level. Open the
vice sufficiently to take in that loop, insert the
thimble, taking care to have it exactly straight,
and screw up the vice as tightly as possible.
Securely fasten the rope and thimble together at
the "neck" A (Fig. 181), when the rope should
appear as there illustrated. Fasten it in the vice

with the thimble hanging downwards, and the part
to be spliced held up by a line suspended from
some convenient joist or girder. Take the whipping off the rope end, and open out the strands
singly, to be ready for tucking. Looking at the
rope from the direction of the arrow A (Fig. 182),
drive a marlinespike through the two strands on
the extreme left, taking care, of course, always to
miss the core of the rope. Twist the spike up the

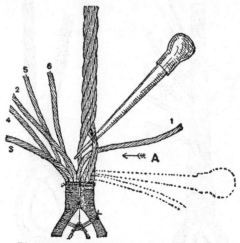

Fig: 182.—Right-handed Splice, First Tuck.

rope about half a turn, so as to make an easier
bend for the strand, then take the strand nearest
the opening, tuck it through, and haul tight.
Then, most important, force down the strand with
the marlinespike till it occupies the position indicated in the dotted lines of Fig. 182.

At the next tuck, with the spike take in the
strand to the right, along with the two just gone
through, making an opening through three strands,
with the point of the spike coming out in the same

place as in the first tuck. Insert the next nearest
end, strand two, and work in snug as before. Of
the three strands the spike has just been through,
take the one nearest to the left, and drive the
spike in so as to make the point come out at the
same opening as before; tuck in No. 3 strand, and
that will make, as in Fig. 183, three strand ends
entering into the same opening in the rope, but
coming out between different strands. After this,

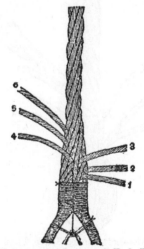

Fig. 183.—Right-handed Splice, all Ends Tucked Once.

simply keep on taking the next strand and the
next end, following round to the left, till all the
ends are tucked once, when an end will come out
between each pair of strands.

The rest is easy. Merely keep on repeating the
operation, with strand and end, until the splice is
long enough and strong enough. As Fig. 180 shows,
after the first set of tucks, it is only a case of each
end twisting and re-twisting round its own particular strand, all the way up. It merely thickens

the strands. After the ends are tucked three or four times, it will make a neater splice if the ends are split and the splice is tapered at the finish by leaving behind one-half of each end, while the other half is tucked once or twice more. Having finished the tucking, take the splice down from the vice, cut off all strand ends quite close, and hammer all down snugly. At the neck put on the

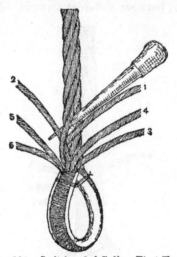

Fig. 184.—Left-handed Splice, First Tuck.

seizing wire, if any, parcel and serve, and .the right-handed eye-splice is complete.

Seizing wire is really a seven-wire strand, made of soft wire, about No. 18 or No. 19 gauge. It is put on a splice for the double purpose of strengthening the splice and rendering it easier to take a weak or broken thimble out of the eye, to be replaced by a stronger one. It is simply bound tightly round the two ropes at the neck, and the end is brought up and round the middle twice or thrice and made secure, as at A (Fig. 180).

Left-handed eye-splicing should be comparatively easy if the preceding instructions on right-handed eye-splicing have been carefully followed Although it is not essential, it makes a neater and a closer splice if a slightly different method of starting is adopted. In splicing a thimble into a crane rope or a trawl-warp, two ropes in which it is very advisable to put left-handed splices, it is

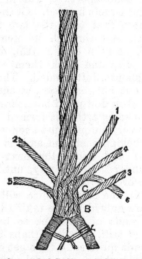

Fig. 185.—Left-handed Splice, all Ends Tucked Once.

unusual to put any seizing on the neck ; instead, the rope is spliced right down to the thimble. Serve sufficient rope to go round the thimble only, leaving out sufficient end for the splice. Turn in and screw up very tight in the vice, make fast at the neck, as before described, fasten the rope up with the thimble hanging downwards, and open out the ends.

Different splicers have different ways of starting, but a very good method is as follows : Turn to Fig. 181, and, taking the strand in the rope nearest the point marked c, open it out with the spike. Select the end that is nearest to it, which will be the inside middle one of the bunch, bring it through to the right hand, as in Fig. 184, and force it down well. Still keeping the spike through the same strand, select the middle strand end, on the outside of the bunch, and put it through the same aperture, but in the opposite direction—that is, left-handed. Of the four strands now remaining, first take the two at the right, and put each end through its nearest strands, right-handed, as at B C (Fig. 185), and the other two at the left, and tuck them through their nearest neighbours, left-handed. There is now an end coming out between each strand, and if the rope is now taken down and hammered well at this part, a very neat starting is formed. All that remains now is very simple; just keep working round to the left, tucking each end as it is reached over its neighbour and under the next one. Work " over and under " all the way, until each end is tucked three or four times.

The appearance of the splice will be improved if the ends are halved before taking the final tuck.

If the strands of the rope to be spliced are very hard and stiff, it will perhaps be difficult to pull in the ends quite snug. To get over this difficulty, before tucking give each strand a sharp bend close to the rope, in the direction in which it has to be tucked, when it will spring into its place with comparatively little pulling. When all the ends are tucked, hammer the splice well, as that makes the wires knit more into one another, and consequently increases the " bite." All that remains now is to cut the ends off, and serve over, finishing at the thimble. It is a good plan to take the splice down now and then during the process of tucking, and hammer it well, as that serves to drive out all the slack at the ends.

Long-splicing is undoubtedly the most important form of splicing. By its use two pieces of rope may be joined together, or a rope may be made endless, without increasing its thickness at the splice. In fact, none but a practised eye can discern where a well-made splice is, after it has been made and set running, as all ends are completely hidden. Ability to splice well in this style commands many good jobs at collieries in this country and in South African mines.

Of course, in long-splicing, as in many other things, different men have different styles. Suppose, for example, a colliery hauling rope is to be spliced, and that it works endless from a hauling engine to a terminal return pulley, mounted on the tension bogie; suppose also that the rope has been put in position, with the ends left at the most convenient place ready for splicing. If 60 ft. of end is available for the splice, decide on that length, and, measuring about 40 ft. from each end, make the rope fast to the rails at one side, and at the other side fix a block and tackle, and haul in every bit of slack lying on the hauling road, taking especial care that the tension bogie is pulled right up to the top of the tension "ways." This is a very important consideration, because if, through the rope stretching, the tension pulley got down to its limit before the rope was worn out, it would necessitate cutting the rope and making a new splice, or opening out the old splice and re-splicing there again after shortening the rope.

Where practicable, have the tension of a sufficient length that by the time it gets to its limit there is sufficient length of rope to make a new splice, in case the old one is found to be giving way. Some ropes stretch more than others in working, and it is difficult to say accurately how much per cent. a rope will stretch, as much depends on the way the rope has been made. However, the larger

the hempen core inside the rope or the shorter
the lay or spiral twist the more the stretch. It
is wise, therefore, when splicing a new rope never
to give any slack away.

Having got the rope hauled as tight as possible,
carefully measure 30 ft. from each end of the rope,
and there tie a strong whipping. It is important
that these whippings should be put on each rope
at a distance which shall ensure that they will
easily come quite up to each other when the two
ends are joined together. Next, take the whippings off the extreme ends of rope and open out
the strands. Some splicers do this in pairs ; others
simply halve the rope, opening it out in two
bunches of three strands each. A better way,
considering laying them in again, is to open out
one strand, then miss one and open out the next
to that, then miss another and take the next one
again.

There are now three single strands opened out
to the whipping at 30 ft. from the end, and between
each of these strands there is one strand unopened.
This work must be done at each end of the rope,
of course. Taking these two bunches of three unopened strands, cut them off about 6 in. from the
whipping and throw them on one side. Open out
the 6 in , obtaining three strands 30 ft. long, and
between each pair is a strand 6 in. long, with the
same length of core projecting through the centre
of the rope. Join the two ends together as in Fig.
178 (p. 135), taking care in every case to have the
strands placed so that a long strand will fall in
where a short one comes out, and at the same time
pull out between the strands the two short pieces
of core A B. Place helpers on each side to pull on
the long strands, as in a tug of war, and after
cutting the two whippings c get the helpers to pull
in opposite directions, until the two ropes are
jammed close up to each other, with the strands
ready to fall naturally into the lay of the rope.
If this is not done properly, or if the rope is

allowed to slip back, the appearance of the finished splice will be spoiled by an unsightly long place in the lay.

Next clamp or securely tie the three long strands at one side to the rope, and proceed to lay the other three long strands into place. Select a long strand and the short one that touches it, open out the short strand, and lay the long one in its place. Keep on doing that until all but 5 ft. of the long strand has been laid in; then stop and lock these two strands together by crossing them, so that they will not open out. Now measure back 5 ft. on the strand just opened out and cut the rest off, as only 5 ft. will be needed on each end. Open out another short strand, at the same time laying in a long one, to the length of 15 ft. only, and the next long strand must be laid in just 5 ft. Now release the other three strands made fast to the rope, and treat them in the same way, laying in a long strand where a short one is taken out. Make all the ends 5 ft. long, putting a small whipping on each before cutting to prevent opening out, when the splice will be as in Fig. 186.

There are now twelve strand ends, 5 ft. long, which must be worked into the inside of the rope and completely hidden; but before this some

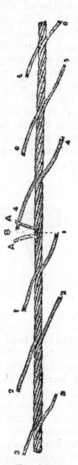

Fig. 186.—
Long Splice,
all Ends ready
for Tucking.

lengths of thin bagging must be prepared, about
2 in. wide, or, failing that, get some thin yarn,
which must be wrapped securely and evenly round
each strand for about 2 ft. or 3 ft. from the end.
Strips of bagging are the better, and can be ex-
peditiously put on by getting each helper to wrap
an end. This gives the outer strands something to
knit or bed into when the hempen core is taken
out of the centre of the rope and the steel strand
ends are worked in. After considering the difference between the size of the hempen core and of
the outer strands, necessitated, of course, by the

Fig. 187.—Making Round Joint.

spiral form of the outer strands, it will be obvious
that the " bite " of the outer on the inner strands
would be very little indeed if the ends were worked
in bare. When all the ends are wrapped and cut
to such a length that they just butt against each
other when worked inside the rope, the work is
ready for tucking. Take hold of the piece of
hempen core A (Fig. 186) and pull it out just to past
the first joint—that is, the two ends 1 and 1'. In
all probability, if the rope is large or rather hard
laid, this will be difficult, unless a tapered round
spike is driven through the two strands immediately behind it.

Strand 1 has now to be worked inside the rope
where the core came out. To do that, take a flat

tucking spike and drive it through the strands
1' and the next one with the point coming out
and covering strand 1. Twist the spike round
in the lay of the rope, and, of course, towards the
original joint B in the splice; but so manipulate
the spike, or "tucker," that strand 1 will fall into
the inside of the rope immediately the worker
starts to twist, as at c (Fig. 187).

When working a strand from the outside to the
inside of a rope it should be done short, sharp,
and at once. Good joints must be made short, for
then the twists in the strands so unite with one
another as to make it appear as though they were
blended into one strand.

The "partner" strand to the one just worked in

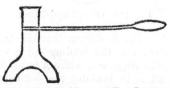

Fig. 188.—Half-round Top Swage.

—that is, strand 1'—must next be tucked out of
sight, but before that can be done it will be
necessary to consider that if the wires in the
strand are spun or twisted in the opposite direction to that in which the rope is "laid" or
"closed," then an ordinary rope is formed. But
if the wires and the strands are both twisted in
the same direction there is formed a make of rope
commonly called a "Langs" or "Albert" laid
rope.

In Figs. 179 to 185 ordinary ropes are illustrated, but in Figs. 178, 186, and 187 Langs ropes
are shown.

In an ordinary rope the strands are tucked
into the inside, side by side at the joint, which is
known as a "flat joint," while in the case of a

Langs rope the strands are crossed over each other at the joint, and this is known as a round joint.

Fig. 187 also illustrates a good way to place the spikes to work in strand 1′ and make a round

Fig. 189.—Wire Rope Clamp.

joint. Each spike is driven through two strands, and, as shown, A is the leading spike which tucks the strand into its place, while B is used simply to combine with A in making the joint and forcing the strand 1′ into the centre of the rope. This is effected by placing the strand between the points of the two spikes and twisting them up in opposite directions. If the spike A is twisted up towards the worker, and spike B in the opposite direction, the obvious result is that the points of the two spikes come down, and simply crush strand 1′ into the centre of the rope. Then go on twisting spike

Fig. 190.—Link Socket.

A along the lay, and spike B can be pulled out as soon as the worker gets away from the joint.

If these joints are closely and neatly made, each in its own way, the two strands forming the joint knit into each other's lay or twist, and will

be scarcely noticeable. The above operation
must, of course, be repeated until all the ends are
tucked into the inside of the rope. Tuck them
in as numbered in Fig. 186, namely 1, 1′, 2, 2′,
and so on. Be very particular in seeing that the

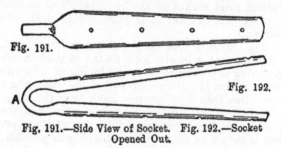

Fig. 191.

Fig. 192.

A

Fig. 191.—Side View of Socket.   Fig. 192.—Socket
Opened Out.

ends exactly butt each other, or a lump results
on the splice; if they do not butt, the outer
strands will sink in. When all the ends are properly tucked, the long splice is practically completed, but it will improve matters to round off
all joints and uneven places with a half-round
top-swage, about the same diameter as the rope.

About all the tools necessary for long splicing
are two flat spikes or tuckers and one round one,
each say 18 in. long, a sledge and set for cutting
the rope and strands, a hand hammer for driving
in the spikes, a strong pair of cutting pliers and

A   B

Fig. 193.—Socket in Wire Rope.

the top-swage (Fig. 188). A very useful wire rope
clamp is shown in Fig. 189.

In addition to the method of fitting attach-
ments to wire ropes by means of splicing, as already described in this chapter, there is the

method of socketing, shoeing, or capping, as it is variously called. There is a great difference between the rough product of the colliery blacksmith, in the shape of the common link socket, and the highly finished cast-steel socket or the turned steel socket of the engineer; and in concluding this chapter it is purposed to deal with them all.

Fig. 190 is a view of the ordinary link socket, often used at collieries as a means of temporarily repairing a broken rope. A whipping of soft wire or spun-yarn is put on each end of the rope, and a few wires then bent sharply back over the whipping and cut off an inch or two shorter than the socket that fits over them. The rest of the rope-end is cut off as close to the whipping as possible,

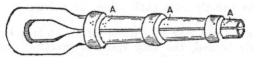

Fig. 194.—Hooped Winding Rope Socket.

and the sockets, which, of course, are ready opened, are put on, hammered down close, and firmly clinched with three rivets.

A very common socket in everyday use is shown by Figs. 191 to 193; this is principally used on haulage ropes and ships' steering-gear. The eye may be of either round or square section, the latter being the strongest and best. As a rule, these sockets are fixed on the rope by means of rivets only, but when attached to winding ropes they are secured with strong steel hoops, which are forged to make a close fit at intermediate distances on the socket, as in Fig. 194.

Sometimes hoops are used in conjunction with rivets. When a hooped socket leaves the blacksmith's shop, the hoops should be a close fit at equal distances on the socket; and as a guide to replacing them correctly, both socket and hoops should be pop-marked with a centre-punch as shown.

The method of preparing the wire rope for these sockets is the same whether hoops or rivets are used. First put a strong wire whipping on the

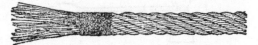

Fig. 195.—Preparing Bulb on Wire Rope End.

rope at about the length of the socket from the rope-end. Untwist the wires of the part left over and straighten them out (see Fig. 195); then bend them sharply back, one or two at a time, over the whipping and over the rope. If the rope has a wire core in the centre, the wires forming it should be bent back the same as the outside wires; but if the core is of hemp, it must be cut off close to the whipping. After hammering snug and close, all these wires have to be cut to a different length, so as to form a tapered bulb corresponding to the tapered cavity inside the socket. Cut the longest wires an inch or two shorter than the length of the socket, measuring from A to B (Fig. 193), and gradually make the other wires shorter and shorter all the way towards the end. These

Fig. 196.—Finished Bulb on Wire Rope End.

wires must now be tightly and closely served with soft copper wire or spun-yarn, using the serving mallet already described in this chapter. For common work spun-yarn is used, and for the best class of work soft copper wire

In bending back the wires, care must be taken

to ensure their being bent equally all round the rope and not merely at the top and bottom or on one side only. The object is to form on the end of the rope a bulb which will completely fill the cavity inside the socket. To do this, the operator

Fig. 197.—Set-hammer for Tightening Hoops.

should work with the closed socket beside him and take the measurement of the inside of the socket at both ends with a pair of inside callipers, and the size of the bulb as it progresses with outside callipers, comparing the two. The socket may have been made rather large inside, in which case it will be necessary to put on two or more layers of serving to bring the bulb to the required size. The rope should then appear as in Fig. 196. The eye of the socket must now be made red-hot.

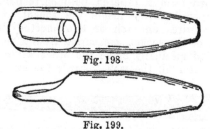

Fig. 198.

Fig. 199.

Figs 198 and 199.—Solid Sockets with Closed Ends.

Cool down all but the extreme back of the eye A (Fig. 192) by the application of water, and open the socket out sufficiently to allow of the bulb being pushed into place. Let the end of the bulb come just to the shoulder A (Fig. 193) of the

socket; then hammer the socket on the anvil, or
screw it up in the vice, until it is as close as it
will go. Cool it down and drive in the rivets,
clinching them well, with a big strong head on

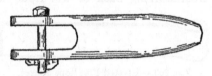

Fig 200.—Plan of Solid Socket with Open End.

each side, for which purpose the holes must be
well countersunk. The rivets should be made of
good riveting iron or of mild steel. A properly
filled socket should show, when finished, a $\frac{1}{8}$-in.
opening between the jaws down its full length on
both sides (see Figs 193 and 194), which would
prove that the socket was properly gripping the
bulb.

When fitting a hooped socket, first pop-mark
the parts, then remove the hoops and thread them

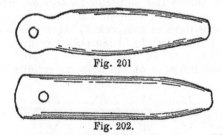

Fig. 201

Fig. 202.

Figs. 201 and 202.—Elevations of Two Forms of Solid
Sockets with Open Ends.

on to the rope, the smallest first and the others
in order; they are thus easily returned to their
proper places. As soon as the hoops are replaced,
the socket should be taken out of the vice and held

end down on a block or anvil while the hoops are driven tightly home with a set hammer (Fig. 197) and sledge.

To give a better finish, and to prevent the hoops from working back or wet from entering,

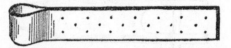

Fig. 203.—Riveted Flat Rope Socket.

they are sometimes caulked on the tapered side ᴀ (Fig. 194) with a caulking set.

For crane ropes or colliery winding ropes, steel sockets are sometimes cast solid, some with closed eyes for the D shackle, as in Figs. 198 and 199, and others with open ends with holes for a slotted pin, as in Figs. 200 to 202, the two latter being side views of alternative shapes. The form shown by Figs. 198 and 199 is the more difficult to fit, as it is obvious that the rope must first be pushed through the socket and brought out at one side of the eye before the bulb can be formed, when it has to be either pulled or hammered back until it is quite tight in the socket. After the bulb of these solid sockets has been pulled or driven into place, it is usual to drive a round tapered copper plug into the core of the bulb, to solidify it and

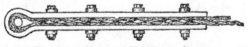

Fig. 204.—Cramped Flat Rope Socket.

increase its grip with the socket. Sometimes molten white metal is poured in to fill up the interstices between the rope and the socket. The hole at the small end of these sockets is made only a very little larger than the diameter of the rope, so that it is impossible for the bulb to pull through if properly made.

Flat wire ropes, which are not much used now, also have to be socketed, as they cannot be spliced. There are various methods of fixing flat rope sockets, varying with the strain and the

Fig. 205.—Socket Cramp.

conditions under which they work. The most usual method is to bend the wire ends back equally on both sides to make the bulb fit the inside of the socket, and to secure with a liberal supply of rivets (see Fig. 203). For stronger work, the rope-end, after being cut off square, is bent round the shackle pin, and the socket made to grip both the rope and its end, the whole being firmly secured by means of strong iron clamps and bolts (see Figs. 204 and 205). In order to drive the rivets through the compressed rope after the socket is tightened, it is necessary to make the way easy for them by driving in tapered spikes of the shape shown by Figs. 206 and 207. These require a hole in the end to take the end of a stout

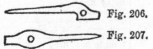

Fig. 206.

Fig. 207.

Figs. 206 and 207.—Riveting Spikes.

Fig. 208.—Rivet.

marlinespike, for the purpose of withdrawing them from the hole. They must be made of mild steel.

The best form of rivet is shown by Fig. 208; it must be made longer than the diameter of the socket, to allow for clinching the other head.

INDEX